S/he

Dress, Body, Culture

Series Editor **Joanne B. Eicher,** *Regents' Professor, University of Minnesota*

Books in this provocative series seek to articulate the connections between culture and dress which is defined here in its broadest possible sense as any modification or supplement to the body. Interdisciplinary in approach, the series highlights the dialogue between identity and dress, cosmetics, coiffure, and body alternations as manifested in practices as varied as plastic surgery, tattooing, and ritual scarification. The series aims, in particular, to analyze the meaning of dress in relation to popular culture and gender issues and will include works grounded in anthropology, sociology, history, art history, literature, and folklore.

ISSN: 1360-466X

Previously published title in the Series

Helen Bradley Foster, *"New Raiments of Self": African American Clothing in the Antebellum South*

DRESS, BODY, CULTURE

S/he
Changing Sex and Changing Clothes

Claudine Griggs

Oxford • New York

First published in 1998 by
Berg
Editorial offices:
150 Cowley Road, Oxford, OX4 1JJ, UK
70 Washington Square South, New York, NY 10012, USA

Berg is an imprint of Oxford International Publishers Ltd.

Library of Congress Cataloging-in-Publication Data
A catalog record for this book is available from the Library of Congress.

British Library Cataloguing-in-Publication Data
A catalogue record for this book is available from the British Library.

ISBN   1 85973 911 3 (Cloth)
       1 85973 916 4 (Paper)

Typeset by JS Typesetting, Wellingborough, Northants.
Printed in the United Kingdom by Biddles Ltd, Guildford and King's Lynn.

Contents

Acknowledgments

I am grateful to the following men and women: Carolyn Ekstrand, for reading the entire manuscript and offering detailed commentary; Robert Morsberger, Ph.D., who reviewed Chapter 1 and introduced me to Berg Publishers; Katharine Morsberger, Ph.D., and Claudie Elmore for their review of Chapter 1; Kathryn Earle and Joanne Eicher, Ph.D., my editors at Berg, who helped convince me that the proposed manuscript might be worthwhile and who responded to my progress reports with good advice; Gerald Leve, MD, for his skill and compassion as a medical practitioner and for offering my questionnaire to many of his patients; C. Jacob Hale, Ph.D., an FTM who taught me about courage; and Jeanne Ebner, founder of the LOTS group, who welcomed me to the monthly meetings. I thank the members of LOTS and their families and friends, whom I cannot mention by name, for the willingness to share their lives with me, sometimes through painful and intimate detail. Thanks to everyone who completed a questionnaire or consented to an interview. I am likewise grateful to the "Under Construction" men's group for allowing me to speak at a meeting and distribute questionnaires. Thank you, all.

Preface

In October 1995, I wrote a letter to a friend, which contained a disturbing but accurate statement of how I viewed my life. When I reexamined this correspondence several weeks later, I was startled by what I had written and that it seemed true at its core. I complained: "After all I've been through with this sex-change thing, I yet hate being transsexual so much that I sometimes can barely stand to look in the mirror. On the bright side, I like being a woman enough that I tolerate my own self-hatred. Hatred is the right term."

Perhaps I was troubled more on this day than others, but perhaps not. The words convey an undertone that I have felt for many years, and readers may be well advised to hold that timbre in mind. I will strive to be objective and accurate as I relate observations, conversations, research, success, disappointment, hope, and despair, but I recognize that my contemplations are personal, even if based on much reading, inquiry, and analysis – and there is my experience as a reluctant transsexual participant in the laboratory of everyday existence. The art of being a sex-changed woman is precarious, and I like to think that I am an innocent student buffeted by too many stouthearted teachers, well-meaning or otherwise, though admittedly the hand that inflicts the heaviest blow is often mine. While I accept my transsexualism as fact, I do not expect that I shall ever be dispassionate about it.

I am not an advocate of sex change procedures. I know that sex reassignment is necessary for some individuals with gender dysphoria in much the same way as a radical mastectomy is necessary for some individuals with breast cancer, but I hope that such treatment is undertaken only when no other effective prescription exists. The best recommendation, though pointless, is don't get cancer and don't be transsexual.

I am a male-to-female transsexual; I have spoken with over a hundred other transsexuals or "possible transsexuals" in the last five years, most in the last two. Some were male-to-female (MTF), some female-to-male (FTM). Sometimes we talked at great length, sometimes briefly. I have met individuals whom I considered well-educated, articulate, feminine, masculine, psychotic, depressed, homosexual, immature, narcissistic, exhibitionistic, flamboyant, reserved, nice, strange, happy, ignorant, naive, sincere, vindictive, alcoholic, successful, unemployable, young, old, witty, dull, and in the middle – much as on a trip to an urban shopping mall – yet what brought me to them was my interest in their struggles with gender identity. I have, likewise, listened to friends, spouses, mothers, fathers, and children of transsexuals pleading their emotional turmoil. Sex reassignment affects many lives.

My investigations do not deal primarily with the roots of transsexualism. Most of my subjects believe that it is something they were born with; but I suppose, like cancer, how one got it isn't nearly as important as managing the problem when one is in its grip. I wanted to look at the process of reassignment, the emotional trauma of growing up with a severe gender/body conflict, and the ways that individuals "accommodate" the disorder through childhood, adolescence, young adulthood, middle age, old age. Related questions include: How are gender-specific dress choices used in the change from one gender role to another? To what degree of success? How must the body be altered to make these dress selections palatable to society and pleasing to the individual? Do patterns change dramatically during the various stages of reassignment? Are the standards inherently different in male-to-female versus female-to-male transitions? To what extent can dress influence third-party perception of gender? How do visible expressions of gender affect identity? Is it strengthened? Is there decreased anxiety? an increased sense of well-being? improved mental health? (as evaluated by the individual and those around him or her). How do transsexuals balance the positive effects of sex reassignment against the negative? Are the idiolects of gender – dress, manner, recognition, and interaction – requisite to identity? How is wearing a certain body like wearing a certain dress?

Beginning in March 1995 I deliberately sought other transsexuals to meet, to know, to understand. For twenty-one years previously, my attitude had been that it was essential to avoid this company in order to protect my identity as Claudine, an average woman by conscious design. I admit that after my first meeting with a group of transsexuals, about forty men and women, I came home nauseated. The emotional pain conjured by the encounter was intensely disturbing, because it was so familiar. I did not want to associate with this malady; I did not want to talk with men who looked like women or women who looked like men; I did not want to see persons in the midst of grave physical transformation; and I did not want others to know that I was transsexual, even others like myself. It took great determination to return to a second meeting and even a third; but by the fifth or sixth, my business turned pleasant, and I looked forward to the second Thursday of each month.

The founder of this organization – Loved Ones of Transsexuals ("LOTS") – is the mother of a transsexual, and I welcomed the perspective of a parent who watched a son become a daughter, struggled with a corresponding emotional discord, yet remains an affectionate mother. (Would I have been so accepting?) Other useful information came from the guest speakers, whom I will occasionally mention, including two speech therapists, a psychologist and teacher, a minister, a social worker, two endocrinologists, a stand-up comedian and image consultant, and a cosmetic surgeon who is one of the few doctors to operate on the vocal cords of male-to-female transsexuals to raise their voices.

I also produced and sent out questionnaires to my physician, Gerald Leve, MD, who has been treating transsexuals since the late 1960s, to see if any of his patients were interested in my research – six contacted me. I handed out questionnaires at three meetings as well, and having found a transsexual anywhere, I always asked if he or she knew others who might talk with me. The response was usually affirmative.

Still, the transsexuals that I met are not a random cross-section. Some are unwilling to risk exposure. Others have adopted a Bowdlerized existence, omitting all references to sex reassignment. Several told me pointedly that they were suspicious of my project and feared that I might intentionally or unintentionally harm them. Some changed their minds from month to month, and I am left wondering if I will ever receive their questionnaire responses or an invitation to chat. The knowledge that I am transsexual did not reassure everyone; others admitted that it was the reason they agreed to meet with me.

My inquiry has not progressed in a deliberate sense beyond these two years, except that I am what I study and cannot escape this scrutiny. Within these limits I gathered more material than was expected. Eighteen completed questionnaires were returned to me from a total circulation of seventy-five; nine respondents were female-to-male; nine were male-to-female. I conducted eleven interviews of two or three hours each, and nine were recorded and transcribed. I met less formally with over a hundred other transsexuals. The most interesting information came when I sat quietly, watching them relate stories, cry, laugh, rave, and interact with family and friends; and, importantly, I observed the transformations of body and manner as several individuals began or "completed" reassignment.

Unless otherwise indicated, quotes from transsexuals or their family members were taken directly from questionnaires, interviews, or conversations. I do not footnote every minor quotation, but generally provide dates and/or locations to add trustworthiness and a time reference for the reader. Pseudonyms are consistent where used, but it is difficult to work with material where almost every primary source demanded anonymity. I offered nothing for the shared experiences of these men and women except the promise that

I would try to tell an honest story, and I have earnestly endeavored to fulfill my bargain. That, in turn, was their gravest demand.

Claudine Griggs

Mind, Body, and Attributed Gender

In *Alice's Adventures In Wonderland*, Alice complains that the Cheshire Cat appears and vanishes so suddenly that it makes one giddy. The cat subsequently accommodates Alice's distress by disappearing ". . . quite slowly, beginning with the end of the tail, and ending with the grin, which remained some time after the rest of it had gone."[1] It is unfortunate that transsexuals cannot fade gently from one sex into the other, but I have found no similar *perceptual* middle ground between male and female as may exist between visibility and invisibility.

There is no intermediate attributed gender.[2] One may see an "effeminate man," "faggot," "he-man," "mannish woman," "dyke," or "Stepford wife," but the person will be perceived as male or female, and from that underlying premise will rise opinions about the displayed qualities of masculinity or femininity. Gender attribution is generally immediate, unconscious, and dimorphic. And it carries contiguous rules about masculine/feminine protocol, which are also immediate, unconscious, and dimorphic.

A transsexual cannot gradually transfigure life from man to woman or woman to man, because s/he cannot be perceived as anything between male and female. During transitional stages, for example, a man may be viewed as a man acting like a woman or trying to be a woman, until at some precise moment, almost as a surprise to the individual undergoing the reassignment, he becomes a woman to those around him. If one is not clearly identified as male or female, that, itself, is conspicuous.

Social pressures change immediately and dramatically when the presumption of man or woman is altered. Depending on an observer's determination, a transsexual may be held to diametrically opposed standards of behavior and dress even where other circumstances are identical. I have even encountered situations while interacting with a group of newly introduced people where I was perceived as a woman by some members of the group and a man by others, with referential confusion until individuals grasped and resolved the apparent conflict.

When I was tenuously perceived as a woman during the first two years of transition, perhaps as one unconfident in or unaccepting of her gender role, I often received lectures on acting like a lady or advice on makeup and dress to enhance my appearance. Sometime it was gentle encouragement, "This will help you look more attractive and feminine," sometimes a warning, "If you don't start acting right you're gonna burn in hell!"

In 1974, a stranger – grandfatherly, perhaps sixty years old – saw me in faded, frayed jeans, and a superbly comfortable sweatshirt at a swap-meet in Pomona, California, and said, "Your daddy oughta turn you over his knee and put you in a dress. Then you'd know how to behave!" In this instance, I was perceived as a woman who was not acceptably feminine. Actually, I was male, 5'5", 120 pounds, with shoulder-length blonde hair, no visible facial hair (preparing for a sex change), walking happily and unselfconsciously around a flea market without consideration that I might be identified as a woman. The absence of feminine apparel did not prevent my being perceived as a female. For this observer, a unisex body in unisex clothes was deciphered as a woman acting like a man.[3] This was offensive.

Another incident occurred while using the men's washroom during this same year. I somehow lost my delicate male image and was seen as a woman by a man who entered soon after I did. He looked at me, glanced around as if to confirm he was in the right place, turned toward me and was about to say something through a growing annoyance. I quickly walked to the urinal, unzipped my pants, and began urinating. The man stared, glancing up and down several times, shook his head in disbelief, and left. A challenged misattribution of gender is emotionally troubling for both parties, and I suspect that this man used the feminine pronoun when referring to me in later recountings of the incident.

Pronoun usage is conclusive regarding attribution, even for people who insult me or insist that I am neither man nor woman. I once overheard two women speak of me in the ladies' room at Chaffey College, neither realizing that I was sitting on the toilet at that moment. The dialogue, which I found interesting even then, was hard to bear:

Jane: I was in here a couple days ago and saw Claudine.
Mary: Really. That's sickening.
Jane: I know. You can tell she's a fucking guy; she's not fooling anybody.
Mary: Yeah. I know. She's sooooooo strange.

These were women I had never met, and who probably heard about my sex change from someone in the campus crowd. They obviously didn't approve, but the feminine pronouns demonstrated their unconscious attribution of gender; the nouns and adjectives, their conscious evaluation of me. Overhearing this *tête-à-tête* four months after I changed my name was peculiarly comforting. I was succeeding as an "attributed" woman, even if general opinion (mine included) held that I was the lowest, most repulsive woman on the planet. — living with ?? diverted at ??

If an observer had to interact with me and could not immediately decipher whether I were male or female, that person would often indirectly ask for clarification. An innocuous "Don't I know you from somewhere?" would elicit a response and allow the observer to hear my voice and manner. Then, depending on the evaluation, that person might be irritated because I was a woman who didn't act like a woman, or a man who didn't act like a man. Contrastingly, young children who were confronted with this same indeterminacy would ask, "Are you a boy or a girl?" They would accept my reply as fact and resume their conversations as if there had been no confusion, although gender attribution changed responsive behavior. Several times, when a young child asked for clarification, I stated, "I am a girl," and the child said, "OK," took my hand, and enthusiastically led me to some game or treasure. When I was perceived as a male, even if I were wearing gender-neutral clothing, children rarely grabbed my hand. And almost without exception, adults who could not form an immediate opinion about my sex were angry: first because they couldn't tell – it's rather perplexing, and several people told me it made them feel "stupid"; second, because I should have dressed or acted more appropriately, which theoretically would have eliminated the confusion.

Life is difficult when one does not have an easily identifiable sex. I found it better to be scorned as an effeminate man or masculine woman than to be sexually indecipherable. But as a result of my temporary ambiguity, I observed the unjudgmental acceptance by children of my reported status, acknowledging that such acceptance came only after the child could not independently determine my gender. This was in contrast to the adult mandate of earning one's place in the world, which led me to understand that visible differentiation of men and women is more important to adults. Children demanded only that they establish my identity as boy or girl; adults required the distinction plus class-appropriate behavior before they could treat me civilly. "Are you a boy or girl?" is a viable question for a child, but as years pass and culturally defined roles are embraced, individuals not only expect clear gender signals, they insist upon them.

Mind and Body Divided

Twenty-five years ago, and many times before, I looked into a mirror and declared with absolute certainty, "That is not me." How could I know? A male image worked fine for everyone else. Their interpretation of my likeness was absolute. With an athletically trained body, a crew-cut, Adidas tennis shoes, Levi's, and a cotton shirt – there was nothing wrong until I stated flatly, "I am a woman." For the observer, the image of gender defines gender; that's the story of the mirror. The reflection is an accessory of self.

In 1997, my hair, earrings, lipstick, mascara, skirt, blouse, shoes, hosiery, and smile look back at me differently, as do jeans, a T-shirt, hiking boots, or even a clean, naked body. There are breasts, a vagina, and a self-attribution of "female." Shadows of a former existence remain mostly in imagination. The reflection speaks comfortingly, "This is right; this is you." Presumably, my inner spirit remains intact.

The predicament of body is in looking though self-identity into the reflection. And when a well-formed feminine gender confronts a well-formed masculine physiology, ornamentation is wrong from the ground up. As a child my body was anomalous, and it could not shake the knowledge: "The mirror lies." Nor, as some seem to expect, did a change of apparel, itself, diminish the sense of wrongness.

At the age of sixteen when I would slip into my mother's clothes, I found no comfort or improvement in the reflection. I would have been perceived as male, and cross-dressing strangely increased my sorrow by reconfirming the incongruity. Years of social training said that I could not don women's clothes. Resultingly, it took much time and self-lecture to convince myself that it was permissible to wear what I wanted, and this turnabout was necessary before I could accept the notion of sex reassignment when proffered by medical professionals. My initial response to a psychologist's suggestion that I begin publicly cross-dressing was, "I can't do that until after surgery. It's not right." This was absurd, since transsexuals generally cannot obtain genital surgery until they have cross-lived for a minimum of one year in the new gender role. But tolerating the sex-change concept was a necessary precursor to modifying my reflection. Later, when I first stepped from my apartment as Claudine, I risked only jeans and a blouse. The image said "woman," barely, but it was a grand difference, and my objective became to improve the reflection through dress, makeup, manner, and feminization of my body.

My sex change was a consequence of war between internal gender and external body, and I defined my enemy bitterly. The battle was further complicated in that I was essentially the only person who knew of the struggle. Victory and defeat occurred when I faced the ultimatum – Become female or die! – and began sex reassignment. But, like Dorian Gray, I anticipated that only the picture would change. I would soon learn that by rearranging likeness, one rearranges audience response, and a radically modified body transforms life experience. Society and self interact with image.

Hormone Replacement Therapy

One of the first steps in gradual alteration of the body for a transsexual is hormone replacement therapy. If the person proceeds with reassignment, HRT will generally continue for the rest of his/her life. Psychological counseling is required before referral to a physician for hormones. The "standards of care" call for a minimum three-month waiting period, but according to Millie Brown, "most therapists wait six months for FTMs [female-to-male trans-sexuals]. These precautions are taken because some of the physical changes resulting from taking male hormones are permanent and irreversible."[4] By contrast, the effects of estrogens on MTFs are usually reversible, at least in the early stages. In addition, almost all the transsexuals I interviewed reported that they had psychological responses to HRT, including an immediate lessening of anxiety in both MTFs and FTMs, mood swings in conjunction with monthly MTF cycles,[5] and increased anger, energy, aggression, libido, and occasional insomnia in the FTMs. Most subjects said that the emotional flux settled after six months to two years.

When I received the first injection of female hormones at the age of twenty, I felt an immediate sense of well-being and calmness. I later told my psychologist, "For the first time, I have something feminine aside from my mind." It was and still is reassuring. This is apparently common among transsexuals, and HRT often provides immediate psychological relief, though it may be weeks or months before the first noticeable physical response. I have even heard transsexuals speak of their "letters," i.e., a psychotherapist's written referral for hormones, with almost the same satisfaction as the treatments themselves.

Soon after a follow-up visit for my second injection of estrogens, I noticed swelling and tenderness in my breasts, and the reassurance was even greater. At last the mirror, ever so slightly, reflected something of me. As months passed and physical changes increased, I grew progressively more comfortable with feminine dress, although it was a couple of months after I had changed my driver's license, social security card, and college records that I found the courage to wear a dress in public for the first time. In many respects the physical evolution regulated my psychological willingness to experiment with feminine expressions.

In the first years of my transition, I equated a feminine role with femaleness, and my initial desire for genital surgery was in part a search for authorial permission to be a woman. The other part was sexual expression. But my psychologist suggested that genital reconstruction in this early period might give me an unfounded psychological endorsement to wear the clothes and manners of a young woman, which might do more harm than good. In retrospect, my doctor was right. It was vital that I unlearn years of social training in how to perform as a male and begin to perform as female, a process that I would have taken less seriously if I had had the operation too soon. My attitude at the age of twenty to twenty-two was that a vagina would automatically bestow femininity. Twenty years later I understand that attributed gender is a handshake contract between observer and observed – it cannot be enforced by genital surgery.

Difficulties of Self-Acceptance

I still engage with the mirror, struggling to see a woman. Self-endorsement of an altered body has been as difficult as changing it, and on certain days I am reluctant to "act" feminine, because I don't feel real. If I put on a red shirtwaist dress, beige pantyhose, black high-heeled pumps, pale rose lipstick, gold earrings, bracelet, and necklace, with gently curled hair, I may responsively feel great, or I may envision an inept drag queen and quickly change into jeans. If duty calls for the dress, I'll bear up, but cringe all day at the image of Hercules in a gay chorus line.

Self-endorsement of ornament and body seems as important as acceptance by others. I was born male. I was raised in rigid Southern Baptist manner as to what was socially appropriate for a boy/man, and I zealously imitated the most conspicuous masculine behavior, censoring even thoughts that I considered feminine. There was no one to teach me how to be a woman or even know that I needed teaching.

Other transsexuals told me that having missed the appropriate childhood and adolescent socialization creates some of their harshest adult struggles, including several long-transitioned FTMs who said specifically that they "feel like an outsider" when among a group of natural males and are still perplexed by the rules of heterosexual dating. They blame the discomfort not on the current physical aspects of their bodies, which they do not minimize, but on their rearing as girls. A present unambiguous physical image can be self-distorted by past images and interactions. These fragments of psychological and physical construction are important, because their alignment, misalignment, or absence affects self-evaluation and the evaluation of others.

Past Attributions in Present Space

In November 1996, I attended my 25-year high school reunion. It was the first time I had seen some of my old friends since I changed identity, although almost everyone was aware that I had been through a sex change. I did not expect to be ridiculed; and in fact, it seemed that people were conscientiously nice to me. I shared cocktails, dinner, dancing, and five hours of conversation; but several disquieting matters surfaced.

An encounter with one of my closest childhood friends, a man whom I've known since fourth grade, went like this:

Friend: Tony, wow! You look nice. It's surprising.
Claudine: Thank you.
Friend: Amazing. I guess I owe you an apology, too.
Claudine: No, you don't.
Friend: No, I do. When I first saw you at Chaffey, I said some things that were pretty cruel. I know it. I'm sorry. But you were so close me, and I couldn't deal with this. I felt betrayed. We were tight as kids, and I just didn't understand all my feelings when you changed.
Claudine: You weren't cruel. I've been in situations that were bad, believe me. You handled yourself very well and exercised a lot of restraint. I know the difference. It hurt. But it was the situation, not you.
Friend: No, no. I said some things I shouldn't. I remember. You remember. Please. I want to apologize.
Claudine: Of course.
Friend: And I have to say your coming here took a lot of guts. More courage than I had back at Chaffey. You're a better man than I am.

My friend's comments were sincere and complimentary. I appreciated them. But no one in my life today would contemplate such a statement, whether I have courage or not. It demonstrates the tyrannical power and permanence of gender attribution. For many people who knew me as Tony, even those who are genuinely sympathetic with my decision for sex reassignment, I am not merely a boy in a dress, I am a boy with breasts and a vagina. If I were pregnant, they would see a man having a baby. They can't help it.

One woman at the reunion told me, "Claudine, you look great! Of course, you were cute in high school. You're still cute." I am certain that she did not mean "pretty," she meant "attractive male." Many friends expressed amazement at how "natural" I looked, but people do not think it is special when a woman looks like a woman. It's uncommon when a man looks like a woman.

Others, especially grammar school classmates, simply could not relate to the person that they met in 1996 as a comrade from 1963. I was *not* Claude

Anthony, I was Claudine – a stranger. In science fiction gradations, I had to convince them that we were really acquainted, relating scenes from fifth or sixth grade. It was reminiscent of the Twilight Zone episode where a man wakes up and his wife doesn't recognize him. So even if I try to acknowledge a whole existence, there remains a peculiar division of life.

In February 1997, I spoke at the University of California Lesbian, Gay, Bisexual, Transgender Association's 8th Annual Conference and General Assembly. It was a three-day symposium, and one of the other speakers was Professor Jacob Hale of California State University, Northridge, who is FTM and whom I will mention several times. A student asked Professor Hale, "How long have you been living full-time?" He responded, "I've been living full-time since the day I was born on July 30, 1958."[6] This is a typical question of transsexuals, meaning "How long has it been since you switched gender roles?" Hale's answer was not typical, however, because he does not separate pre-transition from post-transition being. It's all one river.

But many transsexuals engage in "biographical editing"[7] to make their current lives appear congruent with the past. For example, most FTMs will not admit to co-workers or peers that they were once in the Girl Scouts or had a hysterectomy. Most MTFs will not readily discuss football practice. And I, too, have talked around my life when asked, "Claudine, do you ever have problems with your period?", "How come you've never been married?", or "Do you plan to have children?" These questions are not raised to find out if I'm transsexual; but full answers require disclosure. Some transsexuals invent elaborate personal histories to sustain their current attributions.

The Gendered Voice

Consider the human voice. Men and women sound different. They have distinguishable speech patterns and modulation. In Pygmalion fashion, girls learn to walk and talk like ladies, learn *not* to talk like men. Some dissimilarities are caused by physiological changes at adolescence; others reflect social training and expectation. A woman is obliged to own a womanly voice, one that is of higher pitch, softer, and recognizably different from a man's.

According to Stephen Pincus, MD, there are three important factors that affect the voice: length, tension, and thickness of the vocal cords.[8] Dr Pincus is one of a few doctors who perform surgery to raise the voices of male-to-female transsexuals, which he says is "highly effective" in about 75 per cent of his patients. One of the methods is to stretch the cords, increasing tension and thereby elevating pitch; but the surgical procedure is only one aspect of the transformation.

Lillian Glass, Ph.D., is a speech therapist who works with many of Dr Pincus's patients and who coached Dustin Hoffman for the movie *Tootsie*. Glass landed this role when a producer heard rumors that she "taught men to talk like women." She reports that raising the voice is only one aspect of achieving a feminine speech pattern – women use fewer and less expressive hand gestures, keeping them closer to the body; they speak more softly but with greater modulation, often ending phrases with an upward lilt; their oral communication is punctuated by greater facial expression, especially the smile; and women tend to look others more directly in the eyes when speaking.[9] Without the appropriate mannerisms, the male-to-female transsexual, even with a voice that has been surgically raised to approximate a natural female, may be mistaken for a man, i.e., she will "be read" in public. The ornamental aspects of speech, aside from the actual timbre of the voice, are crucial in overall presentation as man or woman. Genderspeak is more than vocal cords. And the operation to raise pitch is not always effective. Two women reported that they had "unsuccessful" surgeries, leaving them with the same voice problems they had beforehand.[10]

These considerations are applicable to the female-to-male transsexual in reverse, except that in this case, prescribed androgens (male hormones) will cause the female voice to deepen. The vocal cords will thicken and lengthen as they do in natural males during adolescence. This makes a convincing voice easier for FTMs; but mannerisms must change as well. However, my observations suggest that most FTMs have already developed masculine speech patterns before they begin sex reassignment – more staccato in meter, less modulation, even tones, louder, and with more expressive body movement combined with less facial expression – so that once the voice deepens, the overall presentation is unambiguously male.

I personally find that the continual effort of feminine speech is exhausting, and after the first couple of years of living as a woman, I grew resistent to obvious femininity in voice. First, it is troublesome to remember to talk like a "lady" instead of just communicating information without concern for attributed gender, though the corresponding emotional pain of failure in this regard is strong motivation. Second, if I speak with too much inflection, too softly, too daintily, it seems as unnatural as if I make no effort at all and blurt out my words with sports-rally enthusiasm. I like to believe that, when I speak, I speak as a woman because I am a woman; therefore, nothing apart from communication of ideas should be needed. Still, my unguarded oral inflections often deliver sentences like a hillbilly truck driver, and this impresses on some people the idea that I am lesbian. That perception does not bother me.

It can be shatteringly distressing for the MTF who tries to imitate a natural female voice but falls short. I have experienced this and witnessed it. I have also observed individuals, both FTM and MTF, who have vocal presentations indistinguishable from a polished natural voice. When achieved and when contrasted with early recordings of the person, the effect is startling, and it is impossible to associate the individual with the previous voice or attributed gender. According to Lynn Gold, another speech pathologist/therapist who visited the LOTS group, the average female vocal chords vibrate 200 times per second when speaking; the average male, 120 times per second.[11] The difference of 80 cycles per second is generally "sir" or "ma'am." Gold also said that she has never worked with an FTM in speech therapy, "because the hormones they take usually do the job well enough by themselves."[12]

For the natural male or female who grows appropriately into a man or woman, much about gender role is learned without the knowledge that anything has been taught. I suppose it is similar to language acquisition. In many respects, we become boys and girls and later men and women with a similar unconscious ease. Even transsexuals learn the role of their sex, in conflict with gender, because the consequences of not learning are too harsh. So we outwardly adapt to prescriptions that friends, family, teachers, doctors, clerks, textbooks, and even our bodies dictate from the day we are born.

Fortunately, most people, though they strive to become a certain kind of woman or man, never question their foundational gender. If they are female, they are women; if they are male, they are men. They may push at the boundaries of assigned roles, but do not question the assignment itself. Only in rare instances[13] does a male child *know* that she is a girl, maleness notwithstanding. "Female" and "girl" are separate matters; the fact that they are almost always joined together at birth does not change the fact that gender (feminine) and sex (female) are distinct.

My Body, My Enemy

My body became my enemy at an early age. And since the brain is a more important organ than a penis, it became necessary to change my physiology. A male body, with or without clothes, was an inept device for expressing femininity, so I made a better package, one that would allow me to be perceived as a woman. I took female hormones that caused breast development and rearranged bodily proportions – a comforting result. I paid a doctor to remove my penis surgically, which would have been a blessing in itself, and use parts of it to construct the vulva, vagina, and cervix – a painful means to a glorious end. I practiced for years to alter my voice to emulate women and struggled to fit in day-to-day society to earn a living, love, and companionship. If I wear less makeup than some, there are others who wear less than I. If I am less attractive than I'd like to be, I am more attractive than I ever dared hope. If I have suffered much in physical reconstruction, I am at least alive to complain about it; and I have resurrected the tortured spirit of a child grown tenuously into herself.

In 1992, approximately one year after genital surgery and 19 years after I changed my name and social status, I requested a chromosome analysis, spending $885.00 of after-tax money, several hours of time, and a vial of blood to uncover my genetic pattern. Why did I look? After all, it takes sophisticated instruments to see these subliminal infestations. Are transsexuals self-conscious on the cellular level?

Most of that year I suffered a deep depression, which is apparently common after the male-to-female surgery,[14] and I asked my doctor to refer me for a chromosome analysis. He initially hesitated, probing as to why I wanted this, but requested the test "with special attention to mosaicism." Dr Leve was looking for a possible mosaic pattern with a percentage of cells missing the "Y" chromosome, i.e., some normals cells (XY), some abnormal cells (X).[15] I was looking for anything that might help me stomach my troubled bodily image. The specifics didn't matter. I wanted genetic absolution for my transsexualism.

Results: mosaicism was eliminated with a 95 per cent probability, and the karyotype appeared normal for a male, "XY". At times, this knowledge hurts. The cells are female-abnormal, and I hate them individually and in aggregate.

If there exists a lusterless class of people, transsexuals may well be such a group. In *The Naked Civil Servant*, Quentin Crisp, who defined himself as homosexual, writes: "I regarded all heterosexuals, however low, as superior to any homosexual, however noble."[16] My guess is that transsexuals often set themselves another rung below both; and if my observations are accurate, most heterosexuals, gays, and lesbians agree. The feeling of inferiority, not just as woman or man, but as a human being, came to me at an early age and grew to a peak of self-revulsion in early adulthood.

This sense developed in tandem with a growing awareness that there was indeed something wrong with me. It was clear to me and perhaps a few others that I wasn't like most little boys; it was exceptionally clear that I wasn't like other little girls. The difference felt bad.

At the age of six, I first talked directly about my problem with a friend across the street, Danny, another first-grader. I said, "I'm really a girl." This seemed the correct approach – straightforward, honest. Danny's words hurt badly, but his action, worse. He immediately took two steps backwards. I recovered – "It's a joke!" – and all was forgiven.

This tactic didn't work, so several weeks later, in a variation on a theme, I reported to two girls on the playground "I'm a tomgirl," calculating that if tomboys exist, tomgirls must also, and I must be one. That didn't work either, and I regrouped by joining one of the schoolyard armies – no girls allowed – and flourishing in battle. Actions do speak louder than words.

A third strategy was to ask Mother if I had had any kind of operation at birth, hoping that she could explain what I could not. Her response was a perplexed and annoyed, "What on earth are you talking about?" I let it go, deciding at the age of six *never* to discuss the matter again, a promise I kept until the age of twenty. Then I exploded with revelations and began a strange journey. Only a firm understanding that the new path was better than the old enabled me to proceed. When one arrives at the ultimatum, "I must pursue a sex change or commit suicide," something is gained and lost. Reality dictates: "I will never be a natural female. I will be transsexual forever." Such a sentence has consequences.

Sensing Attribution

Because body image is important in establishing attributed gender, I have a peculiar fear of the blind. They must "see" my femininity without visual cues, and I am less confident in these encounters. I rely on physical presence to sustain a feminine attribution.

For three years I lived next door to a blind woman and frequently interacted with her. At my first legal secretarial job in Pomona, California, there was a sightless cashier in the courthouse cafeteria, where I regularly bought a cup of coffee. And one of my fellow students at Chaffey College was blind.

I was terrified each time I spoke with these persons. There never seemed to be a misidentification, but I was afraid, even after they had known me for many months. If people cannot see me, there is little to tell them that I am a woman. A fragrance might help; but I rarely wear perfume. My voice is a clue; but this is my greatest worry.

Imagine yourself in a room, your eyes covered, having a conversation with several individuals whom you have never met. Some voices would be clearly identifiable as male or female, but others, like mine or perhaps naturally mid-ranged, might be ambiguous. How would you determine whether you were interacting with a man or woman? You would listen for content. You would evaluate manner, volume, inflection, tone, number of words between breaths, the amount of laughter, expressed emotion, and, if my experience with blind companions is representative, you would determine with certainty who was man, woman, boy, or girl.

I am more confident when people can see me, because 3-D interaction provides many cues that I am a woman. Even after twenty-three years of practice, perhaps once every few months someone on the phone will say, "Thank you, sir!" I'll be devastated for an hour, and then determinedly re-tune my speech. "Unseeing" encounters still frighten me.

Matching Gender and Sex

Being a sex is important, which is why gender and sex must comfortably match or at least get along to the point where the individual is not destroyed. This is crucial. A person with gender dysphoria is crippled emotionally and socially, which accounts for part of the transsexual compulsion for body alteration.

There is no social pressure for a male living as a man to become a woman. The transsexual belief in "self" over "body" is exclusively personal until such time as psychosocial problems emerge, i.e., an effeminate boy, a tom-boyish girl, depression, self-destructiveness, etc. But initially, instead of expressing gender openly through dress, dating, career, family, and perhaps fantasy, much energy is expended in trying to recreate self as an internal reflection of body – until the psychological crisis becomes too great. Then the transsexual reaches in a variety of ways, perhaps timidly or unconsciously, to become outwardly what she is inwardly.

For myself, the psychological progression developed from the age of two to that of twenty something like this:

> I'm a girl. No, I am crazy. I am a girl in a boy's body. Pain. This is bad, but I can live with it. I want to be female, but so does everybody. I'll join the military and go to Vietnam. That'll make me a man. The armed forces didn't work. Pain. I'll see a psychiatrist and get cured. A sex change? Disgusting. I can kill myself later if it doesn't help. Today's my first estrogen injection. Here we go.

An interesting change occurred once I opted for sex reassignment. I began to worry not solely about becoming a woman, but what kind of woman I was to become. I contemplated vaguely a potential "life."

For the first time, I bought clothes that were appealing to me and wondered: How will I appear in that dress or blouse? What kind of makeup is best? Is that nail polish too dark? Which hairstyle will be complimentary? What work should I do? What should I study in college? I asked other women for advice on dress and manner, practicing their instructions. And on the day that I emerged from my apartment as Claudine, society was quick to inform me when I got it right or wrong.

Once the transsexual steps into a new attribution, he or she is compelled to fit unobtrusively into the corresponding gender role. She is swayed by a desire to be accepted, loved, respected, to have a family, to function professionally, and to feel part of the community – strong motivations. Ironically, many considerations that hold a transsexual from starting reassignment prompt her later to hasten the transition.

According to Holly Devor, "Adults seem almost unable to relate to an 'ungendered' child. When adults are presented with a baby whose sex is not specified, they will generally want to know the sex of the child before commencing social interactions with it."[17] They cannot relate to an ungendered adult either.

As a male-to-female transsexual, the toughest time for me was the transition period (at the age of twenty), when I had started taking estrogens but had not begun living as a woman. It became difficult to identify me as male or female, and since attributed gender precedes interaction, the ambiguity proved frustrating. Society does not appreciate confusion as to which pressures it should convey or which assumptions it can make. Bewilderment brings resentment.

I also discovered that individuals will reprimand a woman who is not appropriately feminine more gently than a man who is inappropriately feminine. A person who is sexually unclassifiable gains the strongest rebuke, and judging by my encounters, ambiguity was almost as hard on the stranger as it was on me.[18] The clearest instruction came swiftly: "Be one sex or the other, and be it quick."

Dressing in Extremes

Many of my interviewed subjects commented that MTFs seem to dress in extremes during their transitions, often wearing stereotypic and/or provocative fashions, overdressing for informal occasions, and wearing clothes that are too youthful for their age. This observation was made by both MTFs and FTMs.

Likewise, my clothing choices fluctuated dramatically during transition. First (on initiation), I tried to match June Cleaver. My dress was crisply ironed, accessories carefully selected, shoes buffed, fingernails manicured and polished, jewelry coordinated, hair and makeup meticulously arranged. I wanted so much to be "normal," to be perceived as female, that I dressed for a yearbook photo almost every day. Second (in rebellion), I mastered the don't-care-how-I-look outfit, for example: faded jeans, baggy T-shirts and sweaters, frayed tennis shoes, drip-dried hair for studied limpness, little or no makeup, no jewelry, nothing that would be obviously feminine. Now, I switch easily between June Cleaver and Dyke Funk.

My "initiation style" was prompted by: (1) the desire to avoid sexual ambiguity; (2) the excitement of finally being able to enter the feminine candy store and sample the wares; and (3) the naive presumption that if I tried hard enough the world would accept my femininity.

The subsequent "jeans mode" developed because: (1) I got tired of always being prim and proper; (2) pants were more comfortable than dresses; (3) I disliked being a sex object; (4) I began to feel as feminine in running shoes as I did in high heels; and (5) my fear of being perceived as a man diminished.

After eight to ten months of living as a woman, I underwent a psychological change. I no longer worried excessively about being accepted as a woman in daily interaction, because it became clear that I would be. I began caring less about everyday appearance, abandoning dresses except for special dates, and sought to simplify my wardrobe. I wanted extra time for work and study, and worried most about how to balance college with economic survival. Career and education became more important than makeup.

By the end of the first year, I would rarely wear a dress or roll my hair, except for the most important occasions, and would arise at 5.00 a.m., shower, comb my long hair straight back and allow it to air dry, throw on pants, a blouse, and shoes, and then study an hour and a half before first class. My attitude: "Forget the frilly crap and finish college." Surprisingly, I turned almost militantly feminist. The traditional female role, especially as expressed through dress, became tantamount to a curse. This I had never before contemplated.

Many MTFs seem to delight in ultra-feminine clothes during the early stages of transition. This is an easy observation. But it is difficult to gauge altered patterns as years progress, for it becomes wellnigh impossible to recognize who is transsexual. Stanley Biber, my surgeon in Trinidad, Colorado, reported that one of his patients is married to a gynecologist who has no idea that his wife is MTF.[19] And all of the FTMs that I've met, except a few who have been taking hormones for less than two years, are absolutely undetectable in clothed appearance.

The group is not easily identified, and information comes from those individuals who wish to be known as transsexuals or at least tolerate it. Some are erratically exhibitionist, but "most transsexuals who make successful transitions disappear and just blend in with the rest of society."[20] The secretiveness of "unreadable" transsexuals can frustrate inquiry on long-term adjustment and dress patterns. Invisibility speaks well of their transition, but it does not favor analysis. Most of the transsexuals that I met at the group meetings were either contemplating transition, beginning transition, or within the first several years of transition. Only a half-dozen individuals had changed attributed gender for a decade or longer.

The Costs of Change

For many transsexuals, the economic situation is grave. They are often disowned by family and abandoned by friends, live alone, and have large medical bills that must be paid in cash. I spent $40,000 during a twenty-year period for professional care directly related to my sex change – psychological counseling, hormone replacement therapy, electrolysis, and genital surgery. The FTM procedure is more expensive, running into six figures for state-of-the-art transformation.

And for MTF travellers, even for those who are successful in obtaining stable employment, it is well documented that women earn less on the average than men. This often translates into an immediate pay cut for a new woman, as it did for me. As many transsexuals are pushed outside the mainstream, they are unable to progress with the transition rapidly. This in turn makes finding good jobs and stable relationships difficult. Extra income is often used to pay medical bills, and many of my subjects reported working long hours, sometimes in two jobs, just to keep up.

Some MTFs work as prostitutes to help pay for sex reassignment. There is a market for pre-op and post-op women, and I was approached three times in 1974–5 regarding such "job opportunities." One man, wearing a traditional suit and tie, overtook me as I left my doctor's office in Beverly Hills, followed me into the elevator, gave me a business card, and invited me to call him for an appointment. You would have thought he was recruiting stenographers. I did not accept, but the offer was tempting. At the time I was literally going hungry to buy hormones.

Gender Role Endorsement

Beauty is an asset. It brings closeness, jobs, monetary reward, love, smiles, warmth from friends and family, stimulating sexual encounters, perceived intelligence, success – and it is fun to accentuate attractiveness. For a woman, beauty brings reward for defined femininity. Clothes, makeup, marriage, and dependence signal a "natural" conformity.

If you are not beautiful or, worse, if you are a male-to-female transsexual who cannot pass inconspicuously as a woman, expression of femininity may bring anger, suspicion, enmity, or violence. An incompetent body colors femininity as a flag of the enemy, and it would seem as implausible for George Bush to wander the streets of Baghdad draped in stars and stripes as it is for a conspicuous transsexual to walk through Exposition Park without drawing hostility. The gardens are the same for all; the regulations are the same; but unequal bodies cannot express gender with equal acceptance, no matter how dear the person.

Self is gendered. The body is an aspect of self. The transsexual who changes roles without successfully altering attribution faces daily insult and misunderstanding. She must also more immutably confront the that's-not-me-in-the-mirror dilemma. *Attributed* gender must be inverted before a transsexual can blend into society and the body can blend into self.

When I am among a group of transsexuals, I am inevitably touched and saddened by their pain, which hangs thickly on body and manner, and which I understand too well. Every interaction with co-workers, doctors, teachers, students, friends, family, and strangers, every kiss, every word, every association is preceded by attributed gender. But attribution is not consensual, and it cannot be rearranged through sympathy. If one is perceived as a man, he will be considered as a man, even if he is Marilyn Monroe psychologically reborn.

Becoming a Woman

I have always had a feminine gender, yet I became a woman not because I changed my driver's license, took estrogens, applied makeup, grew long hair, or had genital surgery, but because on 1 July 1974, a man opened the door for me as I entered my 8.00 a.m. class. It was a powerful culmination of months of preparation and years of inner struggle. I am a woman because everyone who interacts with me says "she" or "her" when they speak of me. My body has become a more accurate display of myself. Without that change, the most feminine attitude, behavior, or dress would not help one person accept me as Claudine. Society must see a woman; otherwise, sex-change surgery or not, one cannot be a woman.

The art of wearing a transitional body is a delicate balance. If a natural female wears a gold bangle bracelet with a pair of jeans and a polyester blouse, "she" is wearing a bracelet. The ornament does not change gender attribution, though it may look attractive, or it may enhance her social status, or perhaps the woman wants to add sparkle to her mood. But for me, especially in the early stages of the sex change, that bracelet often served as a subtle beacon that pushed my perceived status from man to woman.

The collection of signals is important. While I never publicly wore women's clothes prior to 1 July 1974, I did push the limits of ambiguity. The preceding year I let my hair grow to shoulder length. I kept my face shaven. I reduced my weight to about 120 pounds. I spoke softly. I carried my books in my arms. I frequently wore short-sleeved shirts to broadcast that I had no visible upper body hair. But I did not expect to be perceived as a woman; I didn't think it was possible. My intent was to get rid of anything that I considered overtly masculine, guessing that a "neutral" existence would hurt less.

The effects were surprising. First, I was occasionally identified as a woman. Second, the psychiatrist and psychologist I visited in April 1974 both assumed that I had already begun taking estrogens. Ambiguity came easily, and this made gaining a feminine attribution less complicated. I was lucky.

The most grievous problem during this stage, however, was the unpredictability of attribution. I might easily visit a store and be asked, "Yes, ma'am, may I help you?", only to walk two aisles farther and meet, "Sir, did you find everything?" Figuratively, I did not know whether I was a man or a woman until cued by the observer. This is critical information. Believing you are perceived as a man, when you are not, can be embarrassing, disorienting, and dangerous.

For example, when I was twenty, a young man sat next to me on a public bus and, after 15 minutes, without warning, put his arm around my shoulder and tried to feel my breast. This was several months before I started taking estrogens, before I was trying to pass as a woman, before I was even thinking about being *perceived* as a woman. My inner reaction was, "This can't be real! It isn't happening!" All women may occasionally encounter sexual advances they do not want, but it is especially unnerving when a male doesn't realize that he's been perceived as a woman and is thereby a potential object of those advances. The result of this particular encounter was that I got off three stops before my destination and walked the rest of the way; the stranger's response was "Hey, baby, what's your hurry?" I blush even as I type this.

It is troublesome to be seen as a woman when one doesn't expect it, which is a problem that most people never have. They are born male or female and grow into men or women in expectation, conjunction, and general harmony with their bodies. Sex and gender are always concordantly recognized, and the individual always foresees such recognition. But, from the land of intersex, a simple bracelet was sometimes the ornament that allowed me to *expect* to be identified as a woman. And I have in the past worn a bracelet or lipstick, though I particularly like neither, as a measure of insurance against misperception, which was more bothersome than the ornaments themselves. The worst days were when the insurance didn't work.

After twenty-three years of life as a woman, clothes and jewelry have become: What looks nice? What makes me attractive? What is fun? sexy?

proper? comfortable? But during transition, my focus was: What will allow me to be discerned as a woman without getting me beaten up if I should fail in that endeavor? Those were unpromising years for untroubled self-expression through dress. Decisions then were based on three related factors: (1) my anticipated attributed gender; (2) apparel appropriate for that gender; and (3) resulting clothing posture if I guessed wrong at step one.

Observers cannot determine suitability of dress until they are convinced of the sex of the observed. But, within limits, dress can sway the determination of gender (attributed sex comes by default).[21] This in turn affects receptiveness to clothes, hairstyle, manner, voice, makeup or its absence, manicure, jewelry, and role behavior; but the influence of clothing on attribution is less in 1997 than it was in 1974. Before sex reassignment became a "routine" news and talk-show item, gender-specific dress was so firmly engraved in North American society that if someone wore a dress, nylon hosiery, high-heeled pumps, and makeup, it was assumed, except in the most obvious instances, that the person *must* be female. Now, with all variations of cross-dressing (gay, lesbian, transsexual, impersonation, entertainment, and a general expansion of clothing boundaries), it has ironically become more difficult for the MTF to change attribution successfully. If one looks like a man wearing women's clothes, that will be the assumption.

This can have consequences for non-transsexuals, too. We see with Devor's subjects, who were "gender blending" natural females, that they were often perceived as transsexuals or transvestites if they wore traditional clothing:

Seven women disconcertingly found that their particular balance of gender characteristics was such that strangers would think them effeminate men, or men who were trying to pass as women. The women who experienced these mis-identifications found them particularly frustrating because they felt that their efforts to appear as women must be hopelessly inept and useless if they only resulted in them appearing to be gay men, transvestites, or transsexuals.

Two women reported that when they wore dresses, makeup, and jewelry, people thought that they were transvestite men wearing women's clothing.[22]

I met one lesbian, a natural female, who was arrested in the early 1970s for impersonating a woman. "Jan" was certainly boyish-looking, with a boyish manner, but was unmistakably female in my opinion. She calmly related the story, and did not think it was funny.

She had often gone to a bar after work for "a couple of beers." There were many familiar faces, and she talked, laughed, traded jokes, and bantered sports trivia. Two faces belonged to police officers. One day Jan came to the bar directly from her secretarial job, instead of going home to change into jeans and boots, and the officers arrested her. Without success, Jan pleaded that she was female, that she worked as a secretary and wore dresses every day. She had a driver's license, but it was ignored as being "obviously phoney," and she found herself requesting repeatedly from the back seat of a summoned patrol car, "Guys, please don't do this. Please don't do this."

After Jan arrived at the police station, a strip search revealed that she was telling the truth. Jan was female; probably still is.

The power of attributed gender is not to be overcome by dress or a driver's license. Resultingly, surgical techniques and hormone replacement therapy are crucial in assisting transsexuals. The face, body, and voice outweigh clothing. Physiology, itself, must convincingly reflect gender, or gender remains hostilely unperceived.

Professor Hale responded as follows to questions regarding how physical changes allow and/or prevent one from being perceived as a man or woman: "They form part of a 'gestalt' which results in unambiguous, unconscious gender attribution *man* . . . consequently foreclosing gender attributions *woman* or *male-to-female transsexual*. (Female-to-male seems not to be a category available for attribution.)"[23]

Hale classifies "male-to-female transsexual" as a possible attributed gender, which is worth consideration, even if I ultimately reject the concept. The important observation is that there does *not* seem to be a corresponding attribution for the female-to-male transsexual. If one looks like a man wearing women's clothes, that will be the attribution. I define such an attribution as "man," even if the attributor believes the person may be transsexual. Reinforced by Hale's commentary, this will be the case whether the person is an FTM who has not yet achieved an unambiguous masculine attribution or an MTF who has not yet achieved an unambiguous feminine attribution. Women who look like men will be perceived as men, male-to-female transsexuals, or possibly lesbians (still a female attribution), but *not* as female-to-male transsexuals. This bolsters the literature's supposition that there is a tendency to see "male" when ambiguity occurs, with an apparent corollary to see "male-to-female" when the attributor suspects transsexualism. In this regard, I believe Hale's comments accurately describe the hypothetical transsexual attribution.

Ambiguity – Androgyny

Another FTM suggested that "androgyny" may be a possible attribution, distinct from being perceived as man or woman.[24] But again, my experience says that gender neutrality does not precipitate an attribution of "neither male nor female;" it triggers an attribution of "man" from some people and "woman" from others. Ambiguity results in unpredictable attribution, but not specifically non-attribution. Where an observer genuinely cannot determine gender, there will usually be other attempts to decipher bodily presentation through conversational or interactional scrutiny – perhaps direct inquiry – until attribution is made. Additionally, as I describe below, a single observer's evaluation of an androgynous presentation can change quickly.

As I was having lunch in a pizza restaurant in 1977, a new male patron entered and sat beside me at the bar. He ordered a beer. I was likewise drinking beer straight from the bottle and watching a baseball game on the television; I did not select the program, but sporting events are standard fare at barrooms in Southern California. I wore jeans, a football-style jersey shirt, tennis shoes, and no makeup. My hair was down to the middle of my back, but absolutely straight, which was a popular style.

The man began talking to me in rougher-than-normal manner, and it was clear that he perceived me as male. This was several years after I had been living as Claudine, and I had become confident in my ability to express femininity when I wanted. This "new" situation was more interesting than offensive, so I did not protest. After 15 minutes of mundane conversation about the weather, baseball, and how good the beer tasted, the man even jovially slapped me on the back over some innocuous joke. It seemed that he was beginning to think of me as a rather amiable drinking partner. At which time, a male bartender walked over and, speaking to me, asked, "You ready for another beer, hon?" My new friend looked quizzically at me, then at the bartender, glanced around the room as if to confirm that this was not a gay bar, and asked suspiciously, "What do you mean, hon?" The bartender responded firmly, "I always call her 'hon.'" Then I delivered a Miss Georgia smile and leaned back from the counter, allowing the contour of my breasts to show in the dim light.

The man groaned, relieved that the mystery was solved. "Oh, my god. Hon, I'm so sorry. I don't know how, but I thought you were a guy. I can't believe this."

I told him not to worry about it and sauntered to the washroom. When I returned, the man stared intently at me as I crossed the floor and sat again on the barstool next to him. Over the next 30 minutes, his conversation, now gentler and noticeably less abrupt, included: "Gee, I'm sorry . . . I feel terrible. Now that I see you, I don't know how I could possibly have thought . . . But maybe you shouldn't sit so rough, like. You have a beautiful figure . . . And if you didn't put your elbows on the bar, a guy could see . . . Can I buy you a drink? . . . And maybe, I hate to say it, but a little makeup would soften you up . . . I don't know . . . You could fix your hair or something . . . I still don't know how I could be so blind . . .". He apologized for 10 minutes, offering intermixed suggestions on how I could look more feminine. After a while, even I began to wonder if I had carried the "butch" thing too far, though he never used that word.

However, though his perception of me changed from "man" to "woman" in not more than 15 minutes, the attribution was unambiguous at each given moment. I was at first a man who could be slapped on the back over a joke. Later, I was a woman he felt attracted to. The first drink that he bought was partly an apology; the offer of the second (several times) was more than that.

Interestingly, this was one of the few times after I started living as Claudine that I didn't feel sick about being perceived as a man. But also, it was clear to me while this was happening that I was *not* going to be able to sustain that attribution for very long. I knew that as soon as I stood up, my attributed gender would change because my breasts had developed to a degree that was obvious. I could no longer generally be seen as male, but I could, under the right circumstances, be ambiguous, and in this instance that ambiguity, because of the surrounding scene, temporarily garnered a male attribution. I wilfully held it as a self-imposed test. I spoke in fragments and in monotone, shielded my breasts as many FTMs will do, and did not protest after the friendly and painful cuff on the back. My mental reflex was, "You shouldn't hit girls," but I held my tongue. I knew that the "truth" would surface soon enough, and in a way, this was more gratifying than assurances from counselors or friends. It said that I couldn't pass as a man even if I tried. I had been planning to walk to the washroom later on a show-the-bust-and-establish-gender theory, but the bartender beat me to the punch by calling me "hon."

In this instance, there was an unambiguous attribution in spite of an ambiguous presentation. The solid attribution of "man" was brought into question by a third party. That initial attribution was reversed by reexamination of secondary sex characteristics and immediately reinforced by my change in behavior – the big smile.

The birth sex of a child almost invariably aligns with the birth gender. Even males and females who challenge the boundaries of gender role do not question their respective identities as men and women. Prescriptions for dress and manner rigidly follow sex designation, and a gender that stands in opposition to sex generates concern, suspicion, contempt, sometimes pity, sometimes brutality. For the pre-reassigned transsexual, what is appropriate for her psychology will be antagonistic to her friends, family, and strangers as they inevitably reject the perceived incongruity.

Many studies have demonstrated that an established gender identity is immutable; but to alter the body is a desperate undertaking. It is basically reconstructing primary and secondary sex characteristics to match comportment, building the mannequin to fit the dress. Yet if one wants to be perceived as a woman, concordantly unveiling feminine ornament and behavior in whatever ways these are defined, one must simultaneously wear an associated body. It is the difference between: "That dress is all wrong for you!" and "It's wrong for you to wear a dress!" Each statement tells a story about the observer and the observed.

2

Reframing Self

Part-time versus Full-time Femininity

It is difficult to alter the secondary sex characteristics convincingly in most adults, especially if one changes from male to female. Gender role prescriptions may be less rigid in 1997 than they were in 1974, but there is no mistaking a man with long hair and a shaven face for a woman, or a short-haired woman riding a Harley Davidson motorcycle for a man. Once the body has emerged from adolescence, the physical changes confirm sex. According to Money and Ehrhardt, "Gender dimorphism of appearance cannot be successfully abolished after puberty except by people who assiduously cultivate the art of impersonation."[1] Yet even for those who cultivate that art, the inverted gender image is often transitory. An accomplished drag queen may appear meticulously and convincingly female on stage; but off-stage is another matter.

Drag queens in and out of uniform may appear feminine beyond the wildest hopes of many transsexuals. Some have had no cosmetic surgical procedures to accommodate their stage personalities. Others, with the help of electrolysis, breast implants, and facial surgery, though never wanting or pursuing genital reconstruction, effectively become their stage persona and are always perceived as females. They are self-defined as drag queens, but others seem to relate to them emotionally as women. What sets them apart, however, is not their feminine appearance, but their dramatically exaggerated dress and manner, which is not the behavior of women, but a purposefully stylized version of gender role. Natural females who act like drag queens are less entertaining.

It takes effort for an adult male to impersonate a woman, even part-time. But to make the transition from "impersonation" to "being" requires bodily changes that abolish masculine sexual appearance and invert unconscious gender attribution. This can be accomplished with modern medical technology to the degree that, after all that I've been through, I would now have to cultivate the art of impersonation to pass as male. Presumably this would be as difficult for me as for any woman, although I have a voice and some training that could help my performance.

24

Secondary sex characteristics are deemed, like primary characteristics, to reflect gender whether or not this is the case, and transsexuals must alter secondary characteristics so that attributed gender will change from masculine to feminine or vice versa. This is not easy. There is a great difference between impersonation in a drag show – with stage makeup, costumes, complimentary lighting, associated props, and a *willing* audience – and a person's living, working, and interacting as a woman. One cannot successfully "perform" every minute. At some point, the body must sustain its own gendered presentation.

Secondary sex characteristics must be readily accepted in all circumstances as unambiguously male or female, though not necessarily as handsome or beautiful. Attributed gender will be derived on the basis of the immediate and unconscious evaluation of the whole observable package. If a passer-by hesitates for a moment with the thought, "Is that a man or woman?", the transition has not been achieved; on the other hand, if the opinion is, "That woman looks like a man," attributed gender is clearly established, even if the rating is correspondingly low. The gulf between these two assessments is broad for the MTF. One speaks of failure; the other speaks of limited but growing success.

It is apparent that altering secondary sex characteristics is more important than sex reassignment surgery (SRS) as a means of changing attributed gender. Genital reconstruction has little effect on attributed gender, except as it may change hormone levels, especially in MTFs, and thereby modify secondary characteristics over the long run. And I found that changing attributed gender was simultaneously more difficult and more satisfying than SRS. Most of my interviewed subjects agree.

I lived and worked full-time as a woman for seventeen years before having surgery, which, after so long a period, rendered the operation only a moderate statement of femininity. In my responses to the six-month post-operative follow-up questionnaire that I returned to Dr Stanley Biber, I wrote:

> I feel pretty much the same after surgery as I did before. I do not feel particularly more feminine than I did before surgery. I like my body image better. I feel more comfortable with people. I worry less about "being discovered." I feel at ease at the gymnasium. But I had hoped surgery would help me conquer depression quickly and easily; it has not. Perhaps five years down the road, surgery will have enabled me to beat the depression; I don't know.[2]

I wanted genital reconstruction to make me "not transsexual." That did not happen. When I left Trinidad, Colorado, having traded a penis for a vagina, my attributed sex remained female. My secondary sex characteristics were unaffected in the short run, but gradually they became more "feminine," i.e., my breasts started growing again, muscle mass decreased, and body fat shifted. From July 1991, the month of surgery, to June 1996, when I re-checked the proportions, my measurements changed as follows: bust, 36 inches to 39; waist, 28.5 inches to 31.0; hips, 36.0 inches to 38.5, respectively, and I gained almost 15 pounds, then weighing 145, though my diet and exercise remain at close to pre-surgery levels. These changes were facilitated by the reduction of androgen through the removal of my testicles, which continued to produce male hormones in a diminished amount up until the time they were cut away. I continue oral intake of Premarin at the pre-surgery dose of 1.25 mg per day. But over a period of many years, genital surgery or castration in the male-to-female transsexual can affect secondary sex characteristics, but only minimally compared with HRT, electrolysis, thyroid cartilage reduction, rhinoplasty, breast implants, and other cosmetic pro-cedures.

Five years after writing the above-cited passage and almost six years after surgery, I still intermittently fight severe depression. The surgery brought improvement in my life, but it does not compare with the social change from man to woman. My new-found ability in 1974 to express gender openly and to be recognized as a woman – to be myself – marked the critical, life-saving treatment for gender dysphoria. Surgery was pallid by comparison. This is clear in my life, and it has been noted by other transsexuals. Changing attributed gender is the most important step in relieving the dysphoria.

This came as a surprise. When I first contemplated sex reassignment, I viewed surgery as a sanction of femininity, making permissible the expressions I saw in other women. I did not want to live as a woman until after I had obtained surgery; but since my doctors would never have contemplated such an option, I began cross-living as a means to acquiring surgery, not as a means for expressing gender. It was then inconceivable that I would one day describe surgery as a minor addendum in the sex-change process.

Cross-living reduced my emotional suffering and gradually enabled me to express and enjoy femininity. This is not to minimize the frustration of living as a woman with male genitalia or searching for a meaningful relationship in that predicament; but I found a measure of happiness by changing attributed gender. Being a woman with a penis was much better than living as a man.

I worked as a housekeeper, waitress, secretary, and teacher, all of which I basically liked. I attended college and dated several men whom I admired and with whom I had partially satisfying sexual and emotional encounters. I gave up notions of marriage and children early on, and accepted that a pleasant night or weekend with a man was about the best I could hope for.

My friends and co-workers knew me as a woman, and I rarely discussed the fact that I was transsexual – usually only with my doctor or lover. So, compared with my previous existence as a woman who was unrecognizable to anyone but me, this new life was tantamount to a fairy tale. Surgery made life better; but establishing my identity as Claudine made life livable. It gave me a name.

Changing gender attribution requires a collaborative effort of the trans-sexual, medical professionals, and governmental and private institutions. According to information provided by the American Educational Gender Information Service, Inc., and based on the Harry Benjamin International Gender Dysphoria Association, Inc.'s "Standards of Care" for the treatment of gender dysphoria, there are some basic steps in sex reassignment.[3] Harry Benjamin was a New York endocrinologist who wrote the first serious work on transsexualism to appear in the United States, *The Transsexual Phenomenon*, and he popularized the term "transsexualism," which was used by Dr D. O. Cauldwell in 1949.[4]

Guidelines for Sex Reassignment

In 1979, medical providers gathered to set guidelines for treating transsexuals, and they continue to modify the standards of care, most recently in 1990, listing the following incremental steps:

> Diagnosis;
> Referral for hormonal therapy;
> Consultation with an endocrinologist;
> Electrolysis (for MTF patients);
> Cross-living; and
> Sex-reassignment surgery.[5]

Of course, there are additional procedures that many individuals consider, such as facial cosmetic surgery, a tracheal shave (reduction of the Adam's apple), and breast implants, which generally are not recommended until "at least two years after initiation of hormonal therapy, to allow for natural breast development."[6] There is the corresponding removal of breasts for the FTMs, and this is considered "essential" to them.

My first awareness of the formal standards of care came six years ago when I read Kim Stuart's *The Uninvited Dilemma*, and I subsequently found other references to those standards as I read more material in the preparation of this book. I am relieved that transsexuals may rely on a semblance of professionalism and systematic expectations regarding health care. And the diagram of treatment is easily understood, even if its execution is difficult.

When I began living as a woman in 1974, there were no formal standards of care. Just finding a therapist who would work with a transsexual was difficult, let alone obtaining referrals to an endocrinologist and ultimately a surgeon. Transsexuals today expect knowledgeable care. There are still enormous problems in sex reassignment, but individuals have options and advantages I only dreamed of two decades ago. For example, there were no "group meetings" of transsexuals that I ever found. I didn't see another transsexual until two years after I changed my name, and my next encounter was six years later. Now, there are many support groups offering a kind of free counseling from visiting health care workers and "experienced" transsexuals. These groups include: LOTS, Under Construction, Transgender Menace, Genderqueer Boyzzz, Androgyny, Born Free, CHIC, Diablo Valley Girls, ETVC, FTM, Natural Corner, Powder Puffs, the Rainbow Gender Association, and the Society for Second Self. And groups are diverse in philosophy and membership. For example, a flyer concerning Genderqueer Boyzzz offered:

Calling all butches, hermaphrodykes, FTMs, transmen, transboys, transbutches, transfags, transfagdrags, boychicks, girlfags, drag kings, two-spirits, metamorphs, shape-shifters, leatherdyke daddies, leatherdyke boys. Genderqueer Boyzzz is a Southern California social group for people assigned female at birth or in childhood and raised girl-to-woman who have masculine self-identifications some or all of the time. This is a place where difference is treasured. Meetings are open: Everyone is welcome!

By comparison, a handout for "Under Construction" states it "is a men's group . . . designed *exclusively* for the FTM." They only open their meetings to women or "other men" on special occasions.

There are also service organizations and publications that offer information and referrals, including the American Educational Gender Information Service, International Foundation for Gender Education, *A Different Light*, *Cross-Talk*, *Pucker Up*, *T.V. Intimacy*, *Transsexual News Telegraph (TNT)*, *Transsisters*, *Chrysalis Quarterly*, and *TV/TS Tapestry Journal*. Many public and private agencies have established guidelines regarding the documentation for and integration of transitioning individuals. I noticed several years ago, when I was typing documents to request a new birth certificate in an adoption matter, that the state form listed sex-change surgery as one reason for changing information – simply mark the appropriate box. I was surprised and pleased.[7]

Official recognition is a subtle aspect of attributed gender. It helps one believe in gender, which makes its portrayal more convincing; and as rendition gradually becomes reality in the mind of the transsexual, this reinforces self-confidence. It is also a requirement for the real-life test, because in order to live, work, and function in the new role, it is generally necessary to have gender-appropriate identification. Even in 1997, however, not all governments are cooperative, and it remains a crushing blow to me that the State of Tennessee, where I was born, does not allow for a change of birth certificate after sex reassignment.[8]

Let's review again in order the steps listed by the "Standards of Care" for transsexuals.

Diagnosis

This seems sensibly and self-evidently the first item, and it was also my first step in 1974. While no standards of care had then been formally adopted, there were still caring and pioneering professionals willing to assist transsexuals. The second psychiatrist that I visited referred me to a psychologist, who began treatment.

Diagnosis is important, because if one is to rearrange the body for the sake of identity there must be some attempt to understand gender. The therapist is faced with an enormous responsibility in prescribing hormone therapy, cross-living, and ultimately surgery, and in so doing he or she must evaluate gender identity separately from the body that surrounds it. There are psychological tests that rate gender, and I took one when I was first evaluated. But after what seemed a gluttony of scan-tron responses to pointedly mundane questions, the best my doctor could tell me was, "The results seem more feminine than masculine." My own evaluations were more certain, but the psychologist could not assuredly see past my male-body mask.

According to Kim Stuart, "Much of the problem with solving the origins of the dilemma of transsexualism lies in the fact that the condition relates to feelings which are virtually impossible to test with verifiable, empirical evidence ... and the tendency is always to deny what we cannot see."[9] Gender identity is typically defined by attributed gender. Take away an easily recognizable male or female body and the associated dress that accompanies it, and what evidence remains by which the observer can measure gender?

John Money states, "In a sexophobic society, of which our own is an example, extrinsic, nongenital evidence of gender coding is extensively separated or dissociated from the intrinsic evidence of the external genitalia . . . There is a cover assumption . . . that there are absolute criteria against which to define both the extrinsic and intrinsic evidence . . . But there are no absolute standards, only approximations."[10] Extrinsic genitalia may be recognizably absolute, but gender is relative. Further,

> The empirical and objective evidence of transsexualism is provided if the patient passes the two-year, real-life test of becoming socially, economically, and hormonally rehabilitated in the role of the sex of reassignment, prior to the final and irrevocable step of surgery. Gender dysphoria and transsexualism are not perfect synonyms, for there are many gender-dysphoric patients who are not transsexuals, and are not applicants for sex-reassignment surgery.[11]

In other words, the crucial test for gender is the full-time cross-living experience. Treatment confirms diagnosis, and if a male-to-female transsexual *learns* to function successfully as a woman, it must follow that she has a feminine gender, and sex-reassignment surgery can be considered. Kim Stuart expresses a more forceful sentiment on the treatment-is-proof-of-gender issue:

> once a person has lived fulltime (at least one year), has been socially rehabilitated in part, reports happiness in the new sex role, and still wishes sex reassignment surgery (hormone therapy having been given during this period of time), sex reassignment surgery is now indicated and is mandatory. Such persons, after living at least one year in the new sex role, are firmly and irreversibly established in the social role of the new sex. That social role, if successful, validates and confirms their claim to be a psychologic member of the other sex.[12]

Again, it seems that the clinical test for gender in transsexuals is whether or not the individual can live "successfully" in the new role, not measurable criteria from psychological testing. However, the word "successful" as it relates to cross-living has changed dramatically during the last 23 years, so that even that test is dependent on the subjective analysis of the therapist. Someone must decide what constitutes a flourishing man or woman.

This situation is one of the most intensely voiced complaints from transsexuals about therapy, and many harbor animosity toward the prescribed "Standards of Care." Some classify the waiting periods as "prolonging the torture" and resent living to a therapist's definition of what it means to be a man or woman in order to obtain various surgeries. Their solution may be to seek physicians who do not follow or are not aware of the standards. The Standards of Care may appear objective on paper; but subjective evaluations of "intrinsic gender" and "successful role adaptation" are not uniform.

Resentments of the Medical Bureaucracy

To understand some of the resentment transsexuals feel toward psychiatrists and clinics, I offer a brief excerpt of the male-to-female requirements of the "Stanford University Gender Dysphoria Program" that I received in October 1975 in response to my written inquiry; the whole packet included a one-page letter, a three-page program outline, and a twelve-page patient summary questionnaire, which I did not complete at that time:

> Generalized Requirements: . . . The objective . . . is to ensure that each patient proves to herself and society that she can function successfully in the female role. Success is judged by several criteria: (1) Legal identification reflecting the female name and gender; (2) Steady employment as a woman; (3) Absence of sociopathy; (4) Social interaction as a woman, passing and being accepted by friends and family as a normal woman; and (5) Stable lifestyle without evidence of suicide threats and/or attempts or dependence on drugs or alcohol . . . Only patients who have demonstrated successful adjustment to the female role, as judged by psychological, sociological and economic criteria are approved for surgery.

I wonder how many housewives would consider themselves "unsuccessful" in the female role? Why was family acceptance of transsexuals relevant, especially in 1975, when it was much more prevalent for families to reject transsexual members? And, of course, obtaining appropriate legal identification is dependent upon the evaluation and recommendation of the screening psychiatrist. Then there are inherent questions about what it means to be "a normal woman" or "function successfully in the female role." By whose standards? Certainly not the patient's. And if you consider that genital surgery for MTFs was generally acknowledged as one factor in being able to adjust successfully to the "female role," you glimpse the myriad of Catch-22's that transsexuals may confront in their pursuit of sex reassignment – all without guarantee of surgery. Stanford's own estimate was that only "25 percent of those persons who undergo initial evaluation" gained "final approval."

Imagine that you wanted to buy a new car but were told: "You must prove you can be a successful car owner, pay for two years of automobile therapy at $75.00 per hour, practice driving under our supervision, and maintain the Stanford classic image. Then a committee will determine whether you're qualified to buy the car, although we only approve one quarter of the applicants."

Transsexuals feel that they were born with a physical disorder that they have no power to eliminate psychologically. When they are "forced to jump through hoops" by screening medical personnel, many will report false information, saying whatever is deemed necessary to procure treatment without regard for the integrity of the statements. This was frequently described to me, and it has been noted by other researchers as well. Anne Bolin quotes from one of her MTF subjects:

[Psychiatrists and therapists] . . . use you, suck you dry, and tell you their pitiful opinions, and my response is: What right do you have to determine whether I live or die? Ultimately the person you have to answer to is yourself and I think I'm too important to leave my fate up to anyone else. I'll lie my ass off to get what I have to . . . [surgery].[13]

And I discussed the subject with an FTM:

Alex: A lot of the guys are very unhappy with the gender clinics *per se*, and a lot of the gender organizations . . . I think that most of the guys who've had the easiest and most rewarding experiences with therapy have been dealing with therapists that have no experience in this, and they're just dealing with the issues of change and transition, that have nothing to do with the issue of transsexualism, but just how to cope with changes and dynamics within the family . . . I would advise anybody to just find a therapist that they like. Give them the information to educate themselves on their own time. Don't pay them for it. You know, don't be forced to go through the hoops and some of the things that I've had to go through, like therapists.

Claudine: So I'm assuming you felt some resentment . . .

Alex: Incredible amounts. Yeah. The testing and the things that have absolutely no relevance, and paying somebody to educate them and, yeah. Yeah. I've got some real problems with that . . . I think they go a little bit overboard on certain things. And I know, . . . after I had my chest surgery and was living full time for a couple years, and I still, when I entered a new gender clinic, I was forced to take a series of MMPIs. They wanted a psychiatric evaluation. I had to go twice a month. You know, all these things, and it was just like [*grunts*], I was already there.

Claudine: Which you have a feeling is part of their research instead of part of your health?

Alex: Yeah. Right. I don't know if you ever went through that particular one. I'll show you the data base that I was asked to fill out, and never did.[14]

The most severe criticism I encountered regarding "therapy requirements" came in off-camera remarks – succinct and bitter summaries like: "Fuck the psychiatrist. I'm not gonna pay somebody to torture me."

Yet I empathize with the therapist's responsibility. Not everyone who claims to be transsexual is transsexual. Millie Brown lists some of the "others" who may pursue reassignment:

- Gay men or lesbians in denial or confused;
- Transvestites;
- Effeminate men or masculine women who are uncomfortable in gender role but not in gender identity;
- Men with severe erection problems who believe it may be better to be female than impotent;
- Individuals who were sexually abused or assaulted and resultingly find their bodies distasteful;
- Individuals with inappropriate sexual impulses whose fears lead them to seek genital amputation or hormonal castration;
- Criminals who wish to change identity and may seek a sex change to avoid detection and prosecution;
- Individuals with Munchausen syndrome (claiming to have various medical problems in order to get attention, care, and concern);
- Individuals with psychiatric disorders like schizophrenia; and
- Individuals who have multiple personality disorders where one of the personalities may be gender dysphoric even though the others are not.[15]

Inappropriate treatment can be disastrous. The therapist and the real-life test help confirm diagnosis before irreversible steps are taken. I have met one person (MTF) who had had genital surgery and regretted it. She lied to her doctors about having fulfilled the real-life test.

Referral for Hormonal Therapy

After a minimum 90-day evaluation, transsexuals may be referred for hormonal therapy. As I have mentioned, this is an important step psychologically as well as physically. Most transsexuals report a lessening of tension when they begin hormone therapy or even when they receive the written approval for such treatment, often referred to as their "letters." One FTM states:

> Yeah, I guess actually I began the hormones at 29 . . . And, actually, that first shot that I had in Dr Leve's office, I almost passed out, because it was such an emotional thing for me. I mean there wasn't, I wasn't looking for surgery or anything else. That first shot was it. I was going to be a male, after that first shot . . .[16]

I, too, found dramatic emotional relief at the moment I received the first injection of estrogen, though there were no detectable physical effects for about four weeks.

Consultation with an Endocrinologist and Treatment

Hormone therapy is an important step in changing attributed gender; however, it does not provide instantaneous physical effect, and the hormones can cause emotional fluctuations, liver dysfunction, and, after many years, permanent sterility. So persons with gender dysphoria or confusion should work under close supervision of an endocrinologist. One would consider this to be unnecessary advice, but I have met several transsexuals who purchase hormones in Mexico and treat themselves in an attempt to modify secondary sex characteristics. Others told me that they initially stole estrogen pills from their wives.

At a meeting in 1995, I listened to the impassioned pleas for guidance of the daughter (in her early twenties) and the wife (perhaps in her early fifties) of an MTF who was in hospital with liver failure because of self-treatment with hormones. My own endocrinologist mentioned that patients have died from complications associated with liver malfunction related to overdose, sometimes through self-prescription or sometimes as a result of unscrupulous medical providers who will, for a fee, give transsexuals whatever dosage they ask for.

For MTFs, some of the effects of estrogens combined with progestin are: breast development, a slight lessening of body hair (though a male beard must be removed through electrolysis, as hormones will have little effect on facial hair that has already developed), changes in fat distribution plus an increased ratio of body fat, and, possibly, softer, smoother-looking skin. The bodily changes that come from estrogens are generally subtle and unfold over many years. Breast development differs from person to person. Some transsexuals achieve growth that is equivalent to that of natural females; others notice little change. Breast development is not reversible in MTFs once it has occurred. I have heard of "antiandrogens," but have never taken them or known anyone who used them; estrogens and progestins, themselves, have an "antiandrogen" effect and, according to my doctor, this is generally enough to suppress and counteract the body's ability to produce male hormones.

For female-to-male transitions, taking androgens (male hormones) causes a lowering of voice, an increase of body and facial hair, "clitoral growth, increased libido, cessation of menses, and sometimes acne or male pattern baldness."[17] Most FTMs I've talked with also report greater "male sex urges" and more muscle tissue, which they attribute to testosterone and weight-lifting. These effects are apparently pronounced and directly linked to hormone therapy, but I suspect that increased libido is a combination of physiological response to hormones (predominant) and positive social reinforcement of masculine expressions (ancillary). This is based on my discussions with post-transition FTMs, who speak with celebratory pride of their masculinity and sexuality, which they no longer have to hide.

Taking hormones is not without risk, but the risk can be minimized with regular examinations by an endocrinologist – and by following that doctor's advice. I have been taking estrogens for 23 years. During the first year I visited the doctor once each month; over the last 22 years, I have been examined every three months, with blood tests every six months to check for signs of trouble. One common side-effect of prolonged estrogen therapy is a sensitivity to sunlight. My skin blotches easily, and I will burn and blister after about 30 minutes of unprotected exposure during summer.

At one of my appointments with Dr Gerald Leve (2 March 1996), he mentioned that in many European countries, specifically England, Denmark, Sweden, and Norway, where transsexuals are regularly treated for gender dysphoria, there is an approximate 15 per cent rate of severe side-effects from HRT, which he attributes to the more aggressive treatment programs of many European doctors. This contrasts with only one case of "severe" side-effects in his own practice of over 2,800 transsexual patients since 1969. Admittedly, I have heard complaints from many transsexuals who do not appreciate Dr Leve's approach to medicine and complain that he is "much too conservative and cautious" and won't prescribe enough hormones to achieve the desired change in secondary characteristics. And Leve concedes that occasionally patients leave his care and (1) find another physician willing to prescribe higher doses or (2) obtain hormones illegally. This was corroborated by some of my subjects, who buy hormones in Tijuana, Mexico, or who found a practitioner who "isn't so stuffy as Dr Leve." My endocrinologist sadly reported that one of his former patients recently died from a reaction to over-prescribed hormones. Dr Leve discovered this when family members investigating the death inquired as to why the patient left his care in the first place. And my research seems to confirm – through those subjects who traveled to Belgium to have surgery – that European doctors may indeed prescribe higher doses than is typical of California physicians. One MTF who traveled to Europe for SRS said:

Now, I've had a couple of shocks in some ways. The person that was in the bed opposite me when we went to Belgium told me one day. I said, "How much estrogen do you take?" And she said, "Oh, my doctor [prescribes] four or five milligrams." I said, "My god!" I never thought – where I take 1.25, it was five.[18]

For post-op MTFs, the highest reported prescribed dosage of estrogen (Premarin) was a daily average of 1.88 milligrams; this was taken as 1.25 mg one day, alternating with 2.5 mg the next for days 1 through 27, cycling with 5 mg of progestin (Provera) over the last 10 days. Most post-op MTF subjects reported taking 1.25 milligrams of Premarin, generally on days 1–27, 1–26, or 1–28, cycling with 5 mg daily of Provera for the last 7 to 12 days of this period. The highest reported prescribed dose for pre-op MTFs was 3.75 mg of Premarin each day, taken in 1.25 mg doses over the whole day for days 1–27, and usually supplemented by 5 mg of Provera for the last 10 days of that cycle. The highest daily dosage that I ever took prior to surgery was 3.75 mg; most of the time I took 2.5 mg or alternated days with 1.25 mg and 2.5 mg during the 27-day cycle, again with 5 mg of Provera (or its generic substitute, although my doctor still insists on Premarin brand dispensation for estrogen). Since surgery, my daily intake of Premarin is 1.25 mg for days 1–27 plus 5 mg of Provera on days 16–27. I have asked my doctor about reducing the dosage further, which he may prescribe at a later date, because I find the mood swings of the monthly cycle annoying; they are mild but noticeable. I also have corresponding water-weight gain at the end of the cycle, especially during the summer months, which is combined with swelling and tenderness of the breasts – again, mild but bothersome. Similar mood swings and weight gain, which generally occur at the end of their hormone cycles as well, were reported by a number of my MTF subjects. One subject commented that she could tell which week of the month it was by how she felt emotionally.

Corresponding effects of HRT for FTMs that were directly reported to me are: (1) dramatic and immediate increase in libido; (2) cessation of the period after one or two months; (3) enlargement of the clitoris; (4) greater muscle mass and strength (one subject said he used to lift weights five days a week prior to taking hormones, but is stronger now, after five years of HRT, though he hardly ever works out); (5) deepening of voice – most said that they had the familiar adolescent "cracking" during the transition, but two subjects reported a slow, progressive drop without that problem; (6) increase in facial hair and body hair, developing over a period of six months to three years; and (7) elevated aggression, though the few FTMs I watched begin HRT seemed to have about the same aggression levels, but became noticeably more confident in their masculine presentation as the physical effects of the hormones became prominent. Additionally, several subjects reported a decreased need for sleep and higher overall energy levels, which may be related to decreased depression. Some had difficulty with mental concentration during the initial months of treatment, which was sometimes directly related to increased libido, and there was a lower threshold for anger. One man stated: ". . . anger is different. It spikes really quickly, really intense anger, and just drops down to nothing right away again."[19] This sentiment was repeated by several FTMs. About half had some degree of male-pattern baldness, and they generally don't like that aspect of hormone therapy. One FTM was asked pointedly if baldness made him feel more masculine, and he responded: "I accept it as a price to pay, but I could be as much of a man with a full head of hair, and I'd rather have a full head of hair."[20]

None of the transsexuals that I interviewed reported severe unwanted side-effects from taking prescribed hormones, and most noticed no appreciable undesirable results. One woman expressed concern because, after surgery, she has stopped taking all hormones for a period of four years and is too embarrassed to try to find a physician to treat her. This situation came about after her health insurance carrier changed, and she did not want to go to a new doctor and admit that she was transsexual in order to get a prescription. It would also have been more difficult for her to afford the prescriptions under the new coverage. Another MTF developed potentially life-threatening blood clots in her abdomen and legs as a result of unsupervised HRT. She survived a brief hospitalization and subsequently followed a doctor's instructions regarding hormones. Another, who was beginning reassignment, told me vaguely that she had hurt herself "by self-medicating," but later placed herself under the care of an endocrinologist. The highest reported self-prescribed dose of Premarin was 15 mg per day, which is dangerous; two people indicated they "occasionally" took up to 7.5 mg per day.

One interesting problem connected with HRT was reported by Dr Leve. Some MTF patients never see themselves as "feminine enough," even after they have successfully changed attributed gender. They may want more and more estrogen to "feminize" their bodies in much the same way as anorexia patients may want to lose more and more weight.[21] Just as an anorectic woman will view herself as always too fat, the correspondingly obsessed MTF will think she is always being "read." No amount of hormones or feminization will be adequate; consequently, it is incumbent upon the doctor to say "enough."

Electrolysis (for MTF Patients)

Males will need electrolysis treatments to remove facial hair as they prepare for the cross-living experience. Estrogen therapy will not eliminate a beard once it has developed, although there may be some lessening of other body hair. Several methods of hair removal include thermolysis, The Blend, and galvanic electrolysis, and all involve destruction of the hair roots by use of an electric current. The costs for treatment in the male-to-female transsexual average $2,000–8,000[22] and take from one to two years of weekly appointments to complete. According to Millie Brown, electrolysis can cost more than sex reassignment surgery for some individuals.[23] I heard from one transsexual that it took her almost four years of weekly treatments at one hour per session to remove her beard, which was very heavy. It is generally recommended that electrolysis be completed before cross-living begins, because treatment works best when the facial hair is allowed to grow for two to four days between treatments. Electrolysis is reported as "very painful and very expensive." A lot of facial hair must be removed from the average male who wishes to change attributed gender.

I began facial electrolysis ten years after I started living as a woman. I did not need the treatments in order to pass, but gained psychological comfort from not having to shave every couple of days and by eliminating the feel of a stubbled chin and neck. I found "the touch" to be as unappetizing as the look, and removing the facial hair made me feel more feminine and more attractive even though it did not change my attributed gender. But for those individuals with a heavy beard, electrolysis is necessary before the cross-living experience; otherwise, they may encounter the awkward situation of having attributed gender change from its early morning presentation, when they have shaved and applied makeup, to early evening, when a five o'clock shadow peers through even the heaviest foundation. Unlike a drag queen, who must pass for the duration of a show or who may not genuinely attempt to change attributed gender, the MTF seeks to hold a feminine attribution for the entire day – nine hours of work, and then to dinner, the supermarket, a movie, or a social gathering. There is no programmed time limit, and excessive facial hair is a merciless and unrelenting interloper into the life of a transsexual woman. This is true of hirsute natural females as well.

Cross-living

Full-time cross-living is a dream and a curse for transsexuals. The transition may be inevitable and beneficial, but it is disconcerting.

Cross-living is referred to as "the real-life test" among medical care providers. The minimum requirement is one year full-time in the new gender role before sex-reassignment surgery, but most therapists recommend two years, and Gianna Israel advises three to five years.[24] Cross-living is the crux of the "Standards of Care," and I believe it is the most important means of separating transsexuals from those who may confuse transvestism, effeminate male homosexuality, lesbianism, or other identity variations with transsexualism. Only a small percentage of individuals who begin sex reassignment follow through with genital surgery or even continue long-term cross-living. According to Kim Stuart, "about one person in four or five who start the cross living experiment carries forward to the point where they have genital surgery and live the rest of their lives in opposite gender roles."[25]

I met nine people who started the sex-change process during the research for this book. All began taking hormones, often without a doctor's supervision, yet only one FTM has been unwaveringly committed throughout these two years and successfully changed attributed gender full-time. One MTF continues to take hormones and to have electrolysis treatments, but has not yet begun cross-living; she waffles about her decision because of the intense ostracism from her wife and adult children. The others started counseling, hormones, and/or cross-dressing, then stopped, and perhaps started once more, and/or disappeared. Some told me, "This is too hard," and expressed grave concerns over the potential loss of jobs, family, and friends. While cross-living may be an experiment to confirm that a person is transsexual or that sex reassignment may be beneficial, the next step, genital surgery, is *not* an experiment. It is a dramatic and irreversible rearrangement of the body.

Sex Reassignment Surgery (SRS)

I mention this briefly, here, as a designated step in sex reassignment; but it is apparent that genital surgery is not necessary to change attributed gender or many components of gender role. Surgery is crucial to some transsexuals and "low priority" to others; often its relative importance dwindles after attributed gender has been altered for a number of years.

I will discuss sex reassignment surgery more fully in Chapter 4: what it can do, what it can't, and the particular problems confronted by MTFs and FTMs who have had various procedures, their reasons, and surgery's place in the reassignment process. Some of the general admonitions proffered to SRS candidates include: (1) You should be in good physical and mental health; (2) Surgery will not cure all your problems, and most people will treat you just as they did before surgery; (3) It does not guarantee complete sexual pleasure, and results could appear less than convincing; (4) There can be medical complications; (5) There are very few surgeons who perform SRS, so be sure the surgeon is experienced and reputable; and (6) One should expect that the surgeon will require two authorization letters from different therapists[26] – I know personally that Dr Stanley Biber upholds this requirement.

In some states surgery will still not enable one to obtain a new birth certificate. Surgery will not make one "not transsexual," nor will it affect attributed gender. If an MTF has trouble "passing" before SRS, she will have trouble after SRS. Several people confirmed this sad fact, which would seem self-evident, but often came as an unwelcome surprise. Interacting comfortably in society or finding stable employment is dependent on changing attributed gender, not upon the most brilliant genital reconstructive surgery, important as that may be in the overall rehabilitation of transsexuals.

Changing Legal Identity

This is sometimes overlooked as a consideration of attributed gender, even by persons who are undergoing sex reassignment. If one is to live as a man or woman in harmony with gender, one needs the supporting documentation regarding identity that most people take for granted. I have talked with several individuals who have changed attributed gender, have begun cross-living, and yet have a driver's license that reflects their old name and sex designation. I have met some who maintain two separate sets of credit cards – one for the woman, one for the man – to use with alternating attributions. This was a revelation to me, since I changed nearly all my records when I changed my social status. This was a key to having people relate to me as a woman (pleasant) instead of relating to me as a transsexual (unpleasant). It is difficult to change attributed gender and assume an inconspicuous full-time gender role when, as in cases I have heard of, a woman makes a credit purchase in a department store and must display a driver's license bearing a masculine name and a bearded photograph. Reactions vary from sympathy to revulsion to amusement, but attributed gender is undermined in all instances.

When I asked one FTM about the importance of official documentation, our dialogue proceeded as follows:

Mister: Um, it's not primary, but it's important, because what it is is when you present yourself in a certain way, then you kind of, you back it up with official documentation. For instance, if you get pulled over by policeman and you have an ID that is female and you look male, there's a question because of that, or when you start a new job and you present ID that doesn't exactly look like you or it doesn't document it. So it's not the most important thing, but it's very important to follow through on that, to have that documentation to support you after you do a transition.

Claudine: And was it self-assuring just for you?

Mister: Completely. It was self-assuring . . . to finally be recognized officially as this person.

Claudine: Yeah. When I got my driver's license and it said "F" on it, I just felt . . .

Mister: Oh, absolutely!

Claudine: Won-der-ful [*Laughs*].

Mister: Yeah. And when I saw the "M" on mine, I just . . . it was a huge relief as well. And a little more euphoria.
Claudine: And I felt, "Oh, it's so true! It's so true!" [*Both laugh.*]
Mister: And here it is, officially. It's a little nice.[27]

Subtly, and in distinct situations, a driver's license may be a secondary sex characteristic and an element of attributed gender.

Social Recognition of Gender

Displaying Gender through Dress

I did not choose to be a woman, but given that fact, I chose to be female. It was not an easy decision. As a teenager, I often theorized that I could live as a man and suppress gender identity. I was wrong. Consequently, one of the questions I asked other transsexuals was, "Why is it important that others 'see' gender as expressed through your body?"

An MTF responded, "Well, that is the only avenue we have to display gender. It's in the mind, and only its manifestations, such as clothing, are recognizable to other people. Since few transsexuals [MTF] are naturally gorgeous and obviously females, we must give lots of clues. So we tend to fixate on the most obvious marker, clothing."[1] And Jacob Hale (FTM) wrote, ". . . to maintain *my* sense of my*self*, being allowed to move about in the world . . .". When prodded further at a follow-up interview, he added: ". . . I do think a sense of self is relational. And it's not really that I guess that I have some entirely prior-to-interaction sense of self . . .".[2]

Another FTM subject offered:

> I remember a very disturbing point for me, I think in Junior High somewhere, and we were doing the counseling and trying to figure out future careers. And they asked us to see ourselves as a successful adult . . . and all I could see was this three-piece suit. That just like blew me away. I couldn't see myself as a successful adult woman. And at that point I just lost all direction, all motivation. I had no clue as to what I wanted to do, what I wanted to be, anything.[3]

In aggregate these respondents closely represent the summary attitude of most of the transsexuals I interviewed – that even if gender is an inherent quality, and they agree that it is, interactionally it remains dependent on expression. Further, as illustrated by the last-cited respondent, it needs to "be seen" by ourselves as well as others, and even speculation by a seventh-grader hinges on his vision of attributed gender ten years hence. "To be myself" was repeatedly cited as the primary reason for sex reassignment. This interplays with first-person and third-person awareness of body.

I was pleasantly surprised in October 1995 to hear four MTFs calmly debating advice to another who was contemplating genital surgery. There were contrasting opinions about which surgeon did the best aesthetic and functional job, who was the nicest, who charged how much, etc., and I was reminded that the professional care of transsexuals has evolved dramatically in the last twenty years. It seemed that I had searched everywhere from 1975 to 1977 desperately looking for the same procedure, and my yardstick was simple, "Find a willing doctor who won't kill me on the operating table." The thought of choosing among several physicians and picking the best service was incomprehensible; but in 1997 the *availability* of treatment helps in understanding the relationship of body to gender in transsexuals.

This relationship exists for non-transsexuals, too; but as a logical parallel to the way we learn about specific brain functions through the effects of localized cerebral injury, it seems similarly possible to examine various "functions" of gender by looking at the physical changes that transsexuals willfully impose on their bodies and the corresponding points of equilibrium. Some expressions are mandated by gender identity, some by gender role, and others by reproductive physiology; but the three are so tightly and compatibly bound for most normatively gendered males and females that it is difficult to separate them. Transsexualism fragments the alliance.

I and other transsexuals confirm that the most important part of sex reassignment is gaining social recognition of gender, that is, being able to live, work, date, play, and sleep inconspicuously as an attributed man or woman in harmony with the private experience of being man or woman. I mentioned to an FTM that I had "cross-lived" almost twenty years before having genital surgery. He asked why I waited so long, and I reiterated my struggles to find help in the mid-1970s, admitting, "Though I found the situation distressful, I could bear up without surgery because the greater part had been accomplished – I was perceived as a woman. That eliminated 90 per cent of my suffering. The operation was important, but it was not life-saving. My ability to live as a woman was." The man wholeheartedly agreed and said, "Surgery's the icing on the cake." I have heard half a dozen transsexuals describe genital reconstruction as "icing."

Within limits transsexuals can now allow market forces to guide their selection of a surgeon in the "final step" of sex reassignment, which consequentially permits greater flexibility in whether or not they have genital surgery. Those who want it can generally get it. There remain obstacles, but the comparative obtainability of various procedures gives a better picture of how an MTF's vaginoplasty or an FTM's double mastectomy and hysterectomy differ philosophically from a nose job, a tattoo, or orthodontia. I consider that medical treatment for gender dysphoria benefits transsexuals in much the same way that knee-joint replacement assists walking, but with a cosmetic twist.

In *Man & Woman, Boy & Girl*, John Money and Anke A. Ehrhardt eloquently contrast "identity" and "role": "Gender identity is the private experience of gender role, and gender role is the public expression of gender identity."[4] The comparison offers insight into why gender congruency surgery is more than, yet similar to, a nose job, and why altering attributed gender is the more important aspect of sex reassignment.

I have mentioned that when a well-formed gender stands in opposition to a well-formed sex, the affected individual is going to suffer, but that suffering will not always be visible to friends and family. In other words, the public expression of gender may appear untroubled while contravening the private experience. An MTF can play a masculine character to obnoxiousness, excel in rough-and-tumble sports, blast aggression and arrogance, degrade women with bravado, and deliver stereotypic blue-collar insensitivity while hating the acclaimed scenes. I have done it; others have done it. Likewise, an FTM may convincingly play a woman but suffer the performance – one man said that the worst night of his life was when he was crowned homecoming queen in high school. Gender role is not identity for the transsexual.

I asked the question, "What made the manner of dress of your assigned sex at birth 'uncomfortable' for you at various stages in your life?" One FTM wrote, "I felt like I was in drag." A second FTM echoed exactly the same sentiment, and said that he "Always felt 'in drag' in a dress." I heard perhaps a dozen others use similar expressions to describe wearing women's clothes.

My question assumes that the respondents were uncomfortable with the dress of their assigned role. The assumption is generally true for transsexuals; however, the kind of discomfort for MTFs and FTMs is different. Most FTMs "hated" dressing as girls, just as they hated being perceived as girls. The emotions were intense. Most MTFs were relatively neutral about boys' clothes and were disturbed by the prohibition of feminine dress. These layers may intermix, but transsexuals express uneasiness because childhood dress conflicted with their self-concepts as boys or girls, which in turn made the private experience of role uncomfortable. One FTM said that dressing as a ballerina on first-grade Halloween mortified him; an MTF said that not being a princess on Halloween made her feel sick. Two MTFs wrote that boys' or men's clothes were never specifically uncomfortable, but one added that "male clothes only became uncomfortable" after she started "dressing more as a woman," and the other said that she simply likes "to feel well dressed and attractive" as a woman. Again, masculine clothing was essentially irrelevant. Almost all the FTMs reported *strong* aversion to wearing girls' clothes when they were growing up, primarily because it directly opposed their self-identities as boys. It was an insult.

In *Gay, Straight, and In-Between,* John Money defines "drag queen" as the "vernacular name for a male homosexual dressed in women's attire and impersonating a woman, often in an exaggerated way."[5] I have heard self-defined drag queens insist that they don't actually imitate women, but rather the color, energy, sexuality, vitality, and anti-drabness of women, insisting that "full-out drag" is interesting or fun instead of genuinely feminine. Other queens are less flamboyant, but distinguish drag from streetwear. A related question is why does an FTM with a healthy, recognizable, and possibly attractive female body (prior to reassignment) feel "in drag" when forced to wear what would generally be held as traditional dress for a young girl or woman. And why is the FTM uncomfortable in drag even when "she" receives positive reinforcement for dressing like a girl and negative reinforcement for dressing like a boy? Why is the caricature of woman energizing, entertaining, and colorful for a drag queen and bothersome for the female-to-male transsexual? Both define themselves as men, yet part of the answer is that each is a different kind of man.

And to complicate the "drag" concept further, how does one classify the FTM who felt uncomfortable wearing women's clothing before transition, but now, as an attributed man, *enjoys* cross-dressing, i.e., wearing women's clothing? In fact, this particular respondent said that being perceived as a "fag in drag" reaffirms his masculinity. I excerpt a section from my interview with Jacob Hale – he had been taking male hormones for 10 months when we spoke and was/is unambiguously masculine in appearance:

Jacob: And I still have a lot of anxieties about the way my body is at this point, too . . . I only started, only about a month ago, went out in full-out drag for the first time, um, which actually . . . I mean, yeah, it was incredibly affirming to be taken as a fag in drag. And it was just a bunch of fun-delight anyway.

Claudine: So now you're perceived as a man wearing women's clothes?

Jacob: Yeah. Well, not even – that wouldn't be enough. I don't want to be perceived as a man wearing women's clothes. I want to be perceived as a fag doing drag.

Claudine: OK.

Jacob: Very different style. And I don't have the interactions down, yet. Like some of the drag queens are, you know, coming up and talking to me and, "Oh, my name's Ashley. What's yours?" she says, and it's Angelica, and all this. We go back and forth. But I don't have that particular range of interactional styles down.

Claudine: You're still an amateur. [*Laughs.*]

Jacob: Very much an amateur. Not only in how to do the clothes, and I can't do my own makeup. One of my friends did it for me. But I need to learn just how to converse.[6]

Jacob was the only female-to-male transsexual I talked with who admitted any desire to cross-dress as a woman, but he reported that several FTM friends share this pastime. So why is it fun for a genetic female to be perceived as a "fag in drag" after changing attributed gender, but not as a similarly dressed woman beforehand?

Again, a broad distinction about transsexuals is that MTFs don't explicitly dislike living as men. For them, the stress is associated with being denied expression and recognition as women, which their male bodies prohibit. FTMs, however, intensely resent living as women in addition to wanting to express masculinity. (These conclusions are based primarily on my interactions at the group meetings, reinforced by the questionnaire responses and subject interviews.)

For example, one FTM wrote about clothing as follows:

[I was] forced to wear dresses at school, formal situations. I would buy "masculine clothes" myself. Some negative comments about being a tomboy, but mostly left alone – silent disapproval . . . Always headed straight for boy's department – *hated* lace and "slippery things" – dressed very androgynous most of the time, short hair, no make-up . . . Always felt "in drag" in a dress . . . *hated* tights – wanted to always dress comfortably and hated the shoes. Always hated large chest and would wear athletic bras too small, to reduce size . . . never could stand nylon and low cut underwear.[7]

Contrast this with a "typical" response from an MTF about the same issues:

I wore what they [my parents] bought for me. Except for when I cross-dressed in secret. As a young adult I still dressed as I thought I should. The courage to feminize came very slowly . . . [Because of] my obsession with girls and women, I was driven to dress like them. Wearing boy clothes wasn't wrong, it's just that I wanted to dress as a girl . . . When I'm dressed as a girl, especially in public, and I'm functioning, I feel like, "Finally!" as in "What a relief!" I really don't know why. I'm just driven, like wanting something I can't have.[8]

And compare this with Jacob Hale's response when questioned directly on this matter:

Claudine: Well, looking back over it all, would you characterize that you disliked being perceived as a woman or was it that you just really wanted to be perceived as a man?

Jacob: Disliked being, disliked being perceived as a woman. It's more, I, it's more "not woman" than man for me, though not entirely. But more toward that side. I mean, if there were culturally recognized, uh, categories other than man and woman, depending on what they were, I think it is possible that I would be going for one of the other ones.[9]

While it is clear that male-to-female and female-to-male transsexuals both suffer from an inability to express gender openly and from gender attributions that oppose their identities, the anguish is different. FTMs are earnest about dispelling the feminine attribution; MTFs are solemn about gaining it.

A genetic female who feels like a drag queen in a new dress on the first day of kindergarten or high school has a different "private experience of gender role" from a corresponding genetic male who dreams of that same new dress and that same first day of school. And the private experience of identity cannot be "faked" as can its public expression, nor can that private experience be dismantled through the psychological will of the individual. It can be hidden; one can lie about it; but the personal experience is immutable. This was confirmed by *every* transsexual.

There have been many kinds of aversion therapy for gender dysphoric persons, often willingly undertaken and even orchestrated by the victims. According to Kim Stuart: "The treatments which have been tried range from intense psychotherapy, electro-shock, immersion in totally masculine or feminine environments, to hormone therapy. Nothing seems to have worked, and the failure rate is virtually one hundred percent."[10]

It seems clear that the failure is directly related to its attempt to rearrange the private experience of gender role. One might just as well try to cure a natural female who is also a woman of her femininity, or correspondingly relieve a healthy man of his masculinity. If the psychological experience of gender is controlled by the physiology of the brain, as growing evidence suggests,[11] then a rearrangement of that experience will require a rearrangement of physiology. This cannot yet be done, and there are no cerebral blueprints for gender identity. Fortunately for transsexuals, the private experience of role is dependent on identity *and* its public expression. Gender may be fixed, but exhibition is malleable, and the sex-change bargaining table is a workable option for relieving gender dysphoria. This method is well tested.

A change in social status enables the expression of identity. In the eyes of society, a man becomes a woman; for the reassigned individual, an uncomfortable gender role is exchanged for one that feels right, i.e., her private experience becomes internally satisfying. This is not to say that the new public expression will be uniform from individual to individual. I neither have met two MTFs nor two natural females who express gender in exactly the same ways. There may be common ground, but it is a colorful world.

And if gender is predominantly a physiological endowment, one may assume (I think) that there must be individuals who are "borderline" masculine or feminine. As transsexuals initially have "normal" bodies in conflict with "normal" genders, these individuals would have normal bodies with ambiguous genders, perhaps in conflict. However, I consider that gender is not an on/off switch in the same way as male or female, but rather is like a pendulum fixed in motion toward one side or the other. For a person whose gender rests solidly in the feminine range but has a male body, it is an on/off switch, and the conflict may drive that person to sex reassignment. The same is true for a person whose gender is unambiguously masculine but has a female body. But an individual toward gender-middle or perhaps oscillating slightly to either side may not be intensely at odds with either body. And it is the gender/body conflict that creates the dysphoria.

Tremendous effort is required to change attributed gender. Transsexuals universally report that they did almost everything to avoid reassignment, even if they earnestly pursued it once the decision was made. Consequently, it can be assumed that only severe discomfort will push one toward a sex change. The pain must be unrelenting or one will not take the corresponding steps to modify the body, which are disruptive, expensive, painful, and carry potent social consequences. Sex reassignment is not undertaken because one hates to wear a dress at Easter. It is a desperate attempt to relieve grave suffering.

As I have mentioned, by no means everyone who begins reassignment follows through to genital surgery. I pursued a sex change because *not* doing it hurt more. But if this is the case, theoretically there should be individuals who might find some improvement in their "private experience" if they were male instead of female, or vice versa, but are stopped by the difficulty of a sex change. They retain a greater social acceptance, family endorsement, and professional status by intellectually managing the dysphoria. They acquiesce to the sex, attributed gender, and gender role acquired at birth.

Since this book focuses on the transsexual variable in gender, body, and dress, I have not undertaken a systematic search for ambiguous genders. Most transsexuals identify solidly as men or women, though I met some who, having changed attributed gender, declare an "intersex," "bigendered," "ambisextrous," or "transfag" status. There was, however, one notable exception to my non-investigation.

An acquaintance, whom I've known for 11 years and who is a lesbian, has often made comments or behaved in certain ways that made me question her gender. She is 50 years old and five feet seven inches tall, weighs 135 pounds, and is unambiguously feminine in appearance. An accountant by profession, her business apparel generally includes skirted suits, conservative dresses, or upmarket blouses and slacks, without the appearance of "dykeness," though she wears little makeup. And while we had never pointedly addressed gender identity questions, it would not have surprised me if at any time my friend had told me that she was planning to undergo sex reassignment. In any case, as we were discussing the research for this manuscript, I told her, "Based on what I've learned about gender and transsexuals, I would suspect that you are borderline masculine identified, although I don't think you're so out of sync as to go through a sex change." We are close friends, but I expected her to become angry and summarily reject my comments. I assumed that even if the statement were true, she would not admit it. To my surprise, with only a brief hesitation, she said, "I think you're right. But how could you possibly know?" We continued our conversation and she added, "I often feel like a drag queen when I get dressed for work." I had heard her say this once before, and many FTMs say the same thing; it was one of the cues that made me contemplate her core identity as masculine. A year and a half later, she defines herself as a woman but remains intermittently unenthusiastic about that definition. Again, it is the degree of discomfort that prompts reassignment.

Yet, if changing social status is the most important element for transsexuals in achieving a comfortable private experience of gender role, primary sex characteristics are consequential to that experience. Sexual function is a part of gender expression, and genital surgery adds a twist to reassignment that is simultaneously a "public" and a private experience.

There is much debate among transsexuals about the relative value of SRS. Some MTFs don't want it, can't afford it, fear it, doubt it, or accept the concept of a woman with a penis. Many FTMs question the "meaning" of genital surgery because there are so many different procedures, all done in stages (a minimum of three),[12] which may include hysterectomy, vaginectomy, and phalloplasty, with mixed aesthetic and functional results. And FTM concerns that were reported directly to me include: (1) excessive body scarring as skin grafts are taken from the arms, abdomen, and/or thighs; (2) urethral irregularities that promote infections or require regular internal cleaning – one man must clear his urethra each day with a syringe to keep urine from pooling in the base of the penis; (3) pain; (4) inconvenience; (5) general risks of infection; (6) electrolysis on the areas to be used for skin grafts and sometimes around the genitalia before or after surgery – one man said that genital electrolysis was more painful than the surgery and embarrassing besides; and (7) the expense of multiple operations with "experimental" results. In January 1997, one FTM had the first stage of a three-stage procedure that will allow him to stand to urinate. He commented that this is important because of the bonding and "business" that sometimes occur when men enter a washroom and relieve themselves side-by-side at the urinals. Breaking stride to go into a stall while the others remain in the "conference area" is disturbing. Other FTMs said that they won't pay $100,000 for a "settle-for operation," or that they won't risk their ability to have orgasm; and so they live as men with vaginas. I met one 55-year-old MTF who changed identity without hormone therapy or surgery. She tenuously passes as a woman, using clothes, wigs, and makeup to change attributed gender, but is frequently identified as male. She was fired from her job after transition, but says, "This is better than pretending to be a man. And it's better than taking pills or surgery. If I could be a natural female, that would be great. That's not possible, so this will have to do."[13] Again, personal comfort levels and the realities of surgery are considerations.

Unexpressed Sexuality

When I lived as a man, I had no desire to have intercourse with a woman. I likewise had no inclination for a homosexual relationship with a man. Erotic imagery was invariably contingent on my being female, and even during masturbation, whether the object of my desire was man or woman, I could not reach a climax without imagining that I was female. This is still true. When confronted as a teenager by the reality that I was male, my private experience of sexuality was void, and the resulting appetite, or specifically the lack of it, was vaguely questioned by friends, family, and the women I dated. One of my closest high school companions told me that the confusion did not focus on whether I might be homosexual – that would have been understandable – but that I did not seem to be sexual at all. Likewise, it was frequently reported by MTFs that they could not mentally picture themselves as male during a sexual encounter or fantasy; many FTMs could not picture themselves as a female having intercourse with a man.

Experiencing Gender Stereotypes

Elements of the sought-after gender role can cause private discomfort once it is obtained, i.e., most male-to-female transsexuals do not appreciate moving into a world of "second-class citizenship" or being victims of sex discrimination. And while I understood some of the inequities when I lived as a man, it was quite a different matter to experience them firsthand. Some new matters included lower wages and a presumption of stupidity. I was never called a "dumb blonde" as a man, but I have been as a woman, though my hair color and presumably my IQ were unchanged. Being viewed as a sexual object was disturbing, and on a particularly bitter day I complained to my psychologist, "Men consider women as nothing but an orifice for a penis!" I tolerated unwanted sexual advances and couldn't understand why "no" didn't convey "no" after I changed attributed gender. There were bothersome restrictions of feminine dress on the job, and I worked for one employer who required women to wear dresses or skirts every day (and most encourage it, even if the policy is not stated formally).

Contrastingly for FTMs, obtaining the new gender attribution creates social demands in unexpected and not-so-private ways. To illustrate, the following is a brief excerpt from one of my interviews (the subject began a new job after transition, where no one knew that he had previously lived as a woman):

Claudine: Have you noticed differences in the way people treat you at your job?

Mister: You know, that's a good question. I would say that, if I was a real woman in the past, I mean really fru-fru woman, that I would notice a big change. I always was listened to, even when I was, uh, female identified.

Claudine: Yeah.

Mister: I was always listened to. And I spoke, people listened to me. But I would say that the biggest change . . . is that people listen to you more as a male as opposed to female. That when you say something, people shut up and listen.

Claudine: I heard one sociologist, just recently, comment that for men they're assumed competent until proven incompetent, and with women . . .

Mister: Vice versa.

Claudine: They're assumed incompetent until proven competent.

Mister: Till proven competent. I concur completely. And as a female, on my job, I had earned the competence, versus now, I definitely see even when brand new on a job that people listen to me. So.

Claudine: Yeah, I think that's true. I mean, that was certainly my experience. Kind of eye-opening.

Mister: Yeah. It's true. Also, I'm now more physical with people. If something needs to be done that's physical, they just assume that I'll do it.

Claudine: Right.

Mister: Move cases of beer? Oh, Mister is here. [*Laughs.*] No problem. I move tables, chairs. No problem. Mister is here. And before, I would have had ten people helping me. So, I notice less physical help, which is OK, but . . .

Claudine: Yeah. It's part of it. I noticed that the first time somebody wouldn't let me move something after I changed. And I had a flat tire, and somebody

Mister: pulled over and would not let me change the tire, even though I had two lug nuts already off.

Mister: [*Laughs.*] And you certainly could have handled it, I'm sure.

Claudine: Yes, and I could have handled it, but the guy just said, "Oh, you're going to hurt yourself." You know, I've done this before. [*Laughs.*] So it's, it's changed.

Mister: And now it's basically – they expect it.

Claudine: Yeah.

Mister: Now, they expect it. For instance, if there's – and I'm pretty good with this – if something's a little, as, OK, a dish machine is not working. Well, I need to get in there and figure out the problem. It could be a major electrical problem, but I should have a knowledge base, a technical knowledge base. And whether I have or not is irrelevant. I'm a man, so I should, right?[14]

The private experience of role will be affected by the new attributed gender and its corresponding privileges and constraints. That is the purpose of sex reassignment; that is the treatment. But public expression of gender continues to be swayed by approbation or censure, and a new attributed gender is as coercive as the old. This comes as a surprise to many transsexuals. For myself, the overall private experience has greatly improved, but many elements of role remain disturbing.

Attributed gender provides a framework from which dress can be used as an expression of identity. And as one contemplates realignment of body and undertakes physical changes to enter the new role, it becomes necessary to alter dress and manner to function successfully. This task is exciting for most transsexuals, because it is something that they have always wanted. It is also frightening, because they have little training or experience for the inverted expressions.

Prefactorily accepting my gender identity as unalterable and irrepressible was difficult, and it was many years before I could wear women's clothes or even declare a feminine consciousness without expecting some invisible force to strike me or at least call me unprintable names. The first time my psychologist saw me in a dress in late summer 1974, which was the first time I wore a dress in public, he indicated that throughout my session I was sitting "unnaturally still" and using my arms to shield my body. I was aware only that I felt uncomfortable and embarrassed, as if I were cross-dressing and shouldn't be. To others I looked like an appropriately dressed woman; to myself, like a "fag in drag." Learning and unlearning go hand in hand with changing sex characteristics.

As a 14-year-old high school student, when I heard girls complain that they had to wear dresses to school, I remember thinking that no one would ever hear me protest the same. It would be a pleasure to wear a dress each day. Three years later, in my senior year, girls were finally allowed to wear trousers to school – initially during inclement weather only, but later whenever they wanted. My internal reaction was that the new rule would have had no consequence for me, if I were female, because I would never wear pants.

But the reality of a feminine gender role could not be understood, from a feminist perspective or otherwise, until I actually stepped forth as Claudine. In my childhood imagination, I saw dresses and femininity as inseparable, almost as one; today, I see femininity primarily as a state of mind, then as a state of body, and finally, far removed, as a state of dress – though I understand the importance of dress and manner unrelated to the transsexual phenomenon. Dress can emphasize femininity, but it does not create it, and clothing is only one part of existence. It reflects gender-role differences, gender-specific preferences, and gender identity. Dress can also be a burden, whether the person is transsexual or not, if the attendant prohibitions and prescriptions generate discomfort in an individual's private experience. Prior to my sex change, it did not occur to me that role expectations could genuinely annoy normatively gendered men and women.

Knowing the Inner Person

During the research for this book, I found that I was confounded by bodily image when I met a transsexual who was contemplating or just beginning reassignment. Even with my enhanced understanding of transsexualism, I often hoped that these persons would re-evaluate their course, accept their maleness or femaleness, and live respectively as men or women. I was disturbed that they wanted to change sexes.

It is true that life will be easier for the people around transsexuals if the gender dysphoric person can accept body over gender, or at least tolerate it. For the most part, gender dysphoria is not unendurable from one moment to the next, and it is not a suffering that others can see. There was never a day that I hated being male so much that I couldn't survive another 24 hours. What I despised was that it prevented anyone from knowing me. I had no identity but to myself, and the on-going, cumulative pain of *non-existence* drove me to a sex change. And even with my current limitations against full expression of gender, with the prejudice that I have incurred and will incur, my decision was a good one.

Sex reassignment allowed me to display gender acceptably to society and to myself. I will not debate whether it should be so, but when I wore feminine clothes as a child, in private, there was no relief from discomfort, because I appeared in my own eyes to be a boy in a dress and I knew that no one would see or accept my gender. Today, even when I make a conscious and empathetic effort, it is difficult to envision as a woman an MTF who has not had electrolysis, begun hormone therapy, or learned to emulate a feminine voice – gender requires a corresponding representation. But inverting attributed gender is not predominantly about dress, it is about changing the body's perceived suitably for a style of dress. If the body stands in opposition to gender, gender is unrecognizable.

I agree with the previously cited subject that "clothing is a marker of gender" and is "a visible clue for others." But the single clue of dress will not change attributed gender. Attribution comes from a collection of evidence that is readily admissible and congruent to the observer, who may not consciously be aware of all the symbols, but will immediately recognize discrepancies among body, dress, and manner. When attributed gender is altered, the relationship of the "markers" changes. I no longer cross-dress when I put on a skirt; in fact, I do not think in terms of "women's clothes," but rather "clothes." Everything I wear is women's clothes, because a woman wears them.

It is safe to assume that being male or female is a powerful influence that will override or redirect an ambiguous gender in most instances, although defining "ambiguity" would be as uncertain as defining "normative." There have been instances where genetic females have been assigned and reared as boys without resulting gender problems,[15] but it is important to note that when physiological difficulties surface because of the genetic or gonadal sex, appropriate treatment is given to ensure that postnatal physical development aligns with *gender*: for example, if a genetic female with an enlarged clitoris that resembles a penis is reared as male, hormonal and/or surgical treatments safeguard that he will not pass through puberty with menstruation and breast enlargement as a consequence of having internal female reproductive organs. According to John Money, in those cases where adrenogenital syndrome babies were clinically habilitated as girls instead of boys, "it does appear that prenatal hormonal masculinization may have the same long-term sexological effect," and they may both be sexually and romantically attracted to women, but the behavior is socially approved as heterosexual in those raised as male.[16] In these instances, individuals were born with the same genetic karyotype and syndrome, but some were assigned as boys and some as girls. Gender may apparently be swayed toward the sex of rearing, yet some behavioral similarities, such as the erotic attraction to women, may survive. And there were a number of intersexed "male" children assigned as females at birth who nonetheless retained a masculine identity and were reassigned during adolescence as their bodies developed masculine characteristics.[17] Also,

I met one MTF who reported that she was born hermaphroditic but was assigned as male at the option of her parents (more about this in Chapter 6). Thus, sex of rearing may not create a concordant gender in "intersex" brains any more readily than in transsexual brains.

There is a reported case of a child whose penis was accidentally ablated at the age of seven months and who was reassigned and reared as a girl, and this is especially interesting since she had an identical twin brother.[18] Purportedly, the child developed a feminine gender identity, but "had many tomboyish traits, such as abundant physical energy, a high-level of activity, stubbornness, and being often the dominant one in a girls' group."[19] However, evidence is inconclusive regarding the cultural formation of gender in that only a few instances like this have been reported, and obviously medical science cannot create human test subjects as it does with laboratory animals to examine the effects of environment on gender formation; and this particular case has not yet been followed for a lifetime. But certainly, a change in environment for this child, including alteration of her body, first through accident and then through design, affected her psychological development.

In contrast, there is another case of a male infant whose penis was accidentally destroyed at the age of eight months; sex reassignment surgery was performed soon after, giving the child a female anatomy, and the infant was raised as a girl and later received estrogens without being told of the accident.[20] But "Joan" never felt like a girl and was reassigned as male at the age of fourteen, took androgens, and had a mastectomy and phallus construction by sixteen. Dr William Reiner, a child psychiatrist at the Johns Hopkins Hospital, reported "John, in spite of being raised as a girl and being treated with hormones and estrogen, said, 'Forget it. I'm a boy.'"[21] And the mother recalled:

> As soon as he had the surgery, the doctor said I should now start treating him as a girl, doing girl things, and putting him in girl's clothes. But that was a disaster. I put this beautiful little dress on him . . . and he [immediately tried] to rip it off. I think he knew it was a dress and that it was for girls and he wasn't a girl.[22]

Dr Reiner also reports that in adolescent studies of seven males who are being raised as females, two have reverted to being males, and testing on the others indicates a more masculine sexual identity.[23]

As a gender dysphoric teenager "Joan" had a great advantage in having been born male, because her subsequent distress was taken seriously. "She" immediately received treatment and had the support of her family. For transsexuals, instead of gaining assistance from doctors and/or family, efforts are redoubled, often brutally, to make the child conform to gender role of birth. This makes the agony worse. I met several transsexuals who, when suicidal, were told by close family members to "go ahead and do it" because that would be better than a sex change. I, too, was so advised, not only by family members, but by one doctor. Nor are transsexuals "provided" with medical care in adolescence. They must struggle for years to earn money for treatment, and sex reassignment is specifically excluded in medical insurance policies. "Joan" obviously didn't have $150,000 for HRT, a mastectomy, and phalloplasty as a 14-year-old; nor would "her" parents or doctors have consented to it if she had been born female.

Emphasizing Gender

One thing that I have noticed in the studies of reassigned children, through accident or incorrect initial announcement, is a kind of over-compensation in "gender training," which is similar to the enhanced training that many transsexuals who exhibit "problems" get from their parents – an accessory thrust to be sure the children learn to be boys or girls in accordance with assigned sex. For example, regarding the above-referenced accidental ablation of the penis (the identical twin):

> The first items of change were clothes and hairdo. The mother reported: "I started dressing her not in dresses, but, you know, in little pink slacks and frilly blouses . . . and letting her hair grow." A year and six months later, the mother wrote that she had made a special effort at keeping her girl in dresses, almost exclusively, changing any item of clothes into something that was clearly feminine. "I even made all her nightwear into granny gowns and she wears bracelets and hair ribbons." The effects of emphasizing feminine clothing became clearly noticeable in the girl's attitude towards clothes and hairdo one year later, when she was observed to have a clear preference for dresses over slacks and to take pride in her long hair.[24]

I interviewed many transsexuals who report that their inappropriate behavior during childhood, i.e., excessively wearing boys' clothes or being a tomboy for FTMs, or appearing dangerously "unaggressive" for MTFs, brought swift countermeasures from parents or custodial guardians. One MTF reported that not only was she chastised for being effeminate as a child, but in early puberty she was taken to a doctor who gave her supplemental doses of testosterone "to bring out the boy" in her.[25] Another MTF asked her parents if she could be a "girl witch" on Halloween and reported, "My dad had a fit . . . Next week I was enrolled in swimming, baseball, wrestling, whatever was available!"[26] But once the child is able to articulate gender-specific preferences, it is already too late to reshape them.

One interesting matter about very young sex-reassigned children is that the medical professionals never seem to refer to them as transsexual. Regarding the above-cited accidental loss of penis, I find it interesting that the child began life as I did, an apparently normal male, and ended up as I did, a genetic male who is female, yet somehow she escaped the transsexual label and I did not. There is no difference in our chromosomal or morphologic sex, but there is a great difference in our social stature. Despite my never having met the child, who would now be an adult, I would *not* call her transsexual, just a woman; and I am sure that there would be no "visible" clue as to her male beginning, since she was not physically or psychologically disfigured by a male adolescence and enforced masculine role training. Any clue would be specifically related to gender. There are, however, grave social and legal distinctions between this reassigned non-transsexual and me. We are both women, but the judicial outcome is different; self-awareness is different. So at what age does a sex change makes one transsexual – 7 months? (no); 7 years? (probably not); 14? (maybe); 20? (yes, I can attest); 44 or 68? (yes, others can attest). Wherein lies the difference between a sex-reannounced[27] girl and a reassigned male-to-female transsexual? Somewhere in our minds; somewhere in the legal record books; somewhere in our hormonal and physiological development. But I am transsexual and she is not.

Enforcing Gender in Children

It is also interesting that, apparently, when parents try to enforce gender in their children, the emphasis seems to be on "dress" for femininity and "behavior" for masculinity, though not exclusively. As I mentioned regarding the male child reassigned at the age of seven months, the mother made special attempts to keep the child in dresses exclusively and accentuate clothing that was "clearly feminine." Likewise, I've noticed among responses from FTMs that the parents often tried to enforce femininity through a dress code. One female-to-male transsexual writes:

> I was not allowed to buy any boys' pants until I was around 13 . . . I was sent to charm school at age 10–11 to "learn" how to dress and act like a lady but was told I "was hopeless" . . . In tenth grade I tried to wear the "costume" of a feminine girl for the first time but realized it was play acting and that I could not be content this way. [November 1995]

During an interview, another FTM told me of a similarly motivated but self-prescribed attempt to enforce gender when he was a teenager. He first discussed his mother's and grandmother's attempts to make him wear dresses as a child. Then I asked if he ever forced himself:

One time. Because before, I would just stay depressed and do whatever, think of anything else . . . So, one day, and the last time I ever did it, I said, "I'm tired of this mess. I'm tired of feeling this way. I'm gonna stop it, now!" I went home, put on that little nasty skirt suit I had. I can even see the color. It was a maroon type, pinkish type . . ., and I put it on, hideous as it was, legs all nice and cute. Made up my wraggly hair. Put on makeup, which almost made me vomit, but I did it . . . I went out, in public, in a dress, and I felt like a man in a dress. I was totally humiliated. But I did it. I said, "I'm gonna make, I'm gonna stop this. I'm gonna be, I'm gonna make my mom love me once and for all. Hey, this is it!" And the thing that stopped it. I got out of the car – I was going to get some Chapstick. That day is in me. Going to get some Chapstick, and I was walking toward the store, and this man said, "Hey, baby. Have you got a boyfriend?" And that just, pow, I went home, got into my real clothes, and that was the last time I pretended to be female.[28]

Yet for the male-to-female transsexuals who ran into role difficulties with parents and peers, corrective emphasis was placed on behavior, since dress was not generally an issue (most MTFs report wearing women's clothing only in strict secrecy during childhood and adolescence): for instance, the son was enrolled in a variety of competitive sport activities after "he" wanted to dress as a "girl witch" on Halloween. And, again, the transsexual often undertakes corrective action – I talked with several MTFs who joined the military because they believed it would make a man out of them; several believed that marrying a woman and the associated husbandly responsibilities would put their gender problems to rest. Some specifically went all out for sports in high school in the attempt to change gender identity.

I suppose this leads to the question "How does 'dressing like a lady' compare with 'acting like a man'?" Is there an equivalency in forcing a tomboyish girl into stereotypically feminine clothes or sending an effeminate boy to wrestling camp? Part of the problem may come from assuming that dress and behavior are two different matters, instead of contemplating dress as an aspect of deportment. And parental concern for a daughter who wears pants too often is the inverse of a father's dismay that his son isn't aggressive enough. The anxiety stems from a growing awareness that one's little girl may not grow up to be Cinderella or one's little boy into the handsome prince. With severe gender incongruence, the matter is complicated by fear that the son may become Cinderella.

And once more I was struck by a general difference, in that FTMs dislike being held to the dress standards of women and MTFs dislike being excluded from them. This seems to be played out in childhood, adolescence, and adulthood, and in the ways they pursue sex reassignment.

One of the questionnaire items that I usually discussed at interviews was: "After you began to live successfully as a man or woman, how did the social pressures change as far as your dress and/or manners were concerned?" The question that immediately followed, and the question that was more interesting to me, was "Did these changes surprise you? please you? irritate you?"

Eight FTMs responded in their questionnaires that the differences were "pleasing" and "relaxing." One responded, "*Please* is an understatement," and most were enthusiastic about the shift. Likewise, I talked with approximately twenty other FTMs who indicated that the inverted role "pressures" were gratifying and had "a calming effect," despite the otherwise enormous struggles associated with sex reassignment. Only one FTM questionnaire respondent answered that the new social pressures "were and are a source of irritation." This same individual, who had been living as a man for ten years, elaborated that the expectations from some of his peers "to be a male chauvinist and treat women as sex objects" were distasteful, and having previously been a victim of such behavior, he was not about to become a perpetrator. He added angrily, "If that's what it means to be a man, then my image will just have to suffer."[29]

Contrastingly, MTFs reported almost unanimously that they found many new pressures regarding dress and behavior to be disturbing, i.e., "Men expect very little from women mentally. Yes, that irritates me. It also irritates me that all women are supposed to look like fashion models!" Another said simply that it "irritated" her; another that it was "both irritating and pleasing." One, who had been cross-living only a few months, wrote that she was still so surprised to be accepted as a woman that she "felt very good about it." Yet if MTFs find elements of the feminine role annoying, none indicate dissatisfaction with being women, only with the way women are occasionally treated or by the pressures to "be pretty all the time" or "be passive" or "be constantly on display."[30]

Experiences in Being a Woman

When I first changed my attributed gender, I adopted behaviors that were uncomfortable in the private experience of gender role but were generally accepted and encouraged by those around me. Some of these behaviors

......., d me to distraction, and I soon eliminated them; others carried strong social enforcement, and I either conformed to "good-girl" status or bore the consequences. Initially, however, my new-found public expression of gender identity in 1974 focused primarily on achieving a female attribution and willfully adopting its heavily prescribed role. I succeeded beyond expectation, but my definitions of success soon turned sharply. Some highlights of the awakening were:

1. When I first started wearing nail polish, I developed hand and finger movements that I refer to as the proverbial limp-wrist syndrome, which seemed perfectly acceptable to others for an attributed woman, but were not acceptable to me because I considered these gestures as an exaggeration associated with helplessness and incompetence, or perhaps with the gay male stereotype. And it seemed that I developed these mannerisms not by conscious design, but by trying to guard my nails for the 30–40 minutes it would take for the polish to dry: for example, I'd pick up pencils or paper carefully with the pads of my fingers; I would keep my fingers separated so as not to scratch nail on nail; I would hold my fingers straight to prevent "printing" the polish with any other part of my hand; and I would keep my hands away from my body to avoid contact with clothing. These movements habitually carried into the rest of the day, even after the polish dried and the mannerisms served no useful purpose. Six months after I changed social status and to circumvent what I considered a sure sign of "dumb blonde," which had never before concerned me, I quit wearing nail polish. I never missed it, though I recognize that many women enjoy intermittent visits to a salon to have their nails manicured and lacquered, or to have acrylic nails applied, without feeling self-conscious about the counterbalancing gestures that accompany this ritual. I have often received advice to do my nails from peers.

2. There was a sense of defenselessness associated with many articles of feminine dress. In *Passage through Trinidad*, regarding my selection of clothes for a meeting with a genetics counselor, I wrote:

> I decided to wear Levi's 501 blue jeans, a simple shirt-style white blouse, a tan corduroy sports jacket, white Nike running shoes, and no jewelry. I have adopted a "neutral" mode of dress, wearing nothing that is specifically feminine, other than my purse and customary underclothes. I've always felt peculiarly ill at ease when dressing to meet for the first time someone who knows that I'm trans-sexual.

> After almost 18 years as Claudine, I still opt for gender-neutral clothing in these situations to (1) prove that I don't need "feminine" clothes to pass as female, (2) assert that underneath my somewhat delicate exterior I can be "butch" if necessary, (3) help put the other person at ease, and (4) put myself at ease – it has always

seemed less difficult to handle insults and/or awkward situations while wearing a T-shirt, jeans, and tennis shoes, as opposed to high-heeled pumps and a miniskirt.[31]

Soon after changing attributed gender, I discovered that there is a physical and psychological restrictiveness to some feminine dress. Gradually, as I became comfortable wearing women's clothes, I experimented with more stereotypic attire. It was and is difficult for me to feel bold while wearing a short, tight-fitting skirt and tottering about on high heels. Four or five months after I changed attributed gender, as students at Chaffey College discovered that there was a transsexual among them, I generally shifted to jeans, low-heeled walking shoes, and sweaters or man-style blouses, because I could at any time meet with hostile confrontation. Showdowns rarely happened on campus, but a few instances made me wary. (Everything considered, I give my fellow students much credit for understanding and compassion. I often expect the worst but rarely get it.)

Not only did I feel weaker and less physically capable in dresses and heels, but I found that I would additionally project that on to other women, and they to me. If I were with a group of four women and we walked into the cafeteria, the one who was the most femininely dressed would invariably pass the threshold with another holding the door. This appeared independent of my status as a transsexual woman for those who knew about me, but was rather a function of how I dressed. If I wore what I then called "a hunting outfit," a man's attention being the prey, my female friends – all in their early twenties – would generally show me the same consideration about opening doors as a man; if I were in a functional mode or my later-developed, I-hate-dresses stage, I found myself unconsciously assuming a higher door-opening authority; again, among a group of women. Put one man among us, and he would hold the door for all regardless of how we were dressed.

Along these lines, I began a new secretarial job in December 1994 just as the business was preparing to relocate; resultingly, I spent several days packing, indexing, and stacking file storage boxes. It was heavy work, and I wore pants and even brought a pair of gloves to protect my hands from the repetitive push, pull, lift, stack, all without any apparent concern from my employer. But on the last workday before the Christmas holiday, I wore a red dress of delicate fabric and black medium-heeled pumps, with a gold bracelet and earrings. On that day, my employer questioned whether I was comfortable doing such unwieldy labor. My dress was not physically restrictive; I specifically selected it for its full range of movement. But there were psychological implications. My boss seemed to notice for the first time that I was a woman lifting boxes. In turn, I became self-conscious about my activity or soiling my clothing, which was wash-and-wear polyester. I don't believe that dress predominantly affects core gender or gender attribution, but it appears to affect the way I and others evaluate gender role and its boundaries. A woman who presents an ultra-feminine style is likely to receive encouragement and expectation to conform to that image; a woman who dresses in an understated fashion is more likely to be unnoticed if she is moving heavy cartons. Some of the invisible lines surrounding gender roles become visible when crossed.

3. Gender-specific dress was more time-consuming as a woman than it had been as a man; in fact, there was much more gender-specific dress associated with the feminine role. Putting on foundation, mascara, and lipstick, curling my hair, polishing my nails, climbing into pantyhose and a skirt each morning before class, then changing into jeans each afternoon as I hurried off to clean house for a family in Claremont reduced the available hours for work and study. The morning ritual of accentuating a quaking feminine attributed gender (and I was not confident about my daily success) took me about an hour and a half. My male ceremony took twenty minutes. The disparity was disturbing.

4. An unambiguous gender identity did not automatically grant success in gender role.

I wanted to go to college; I needed a job to earn money for food, shelter, medical care, books, and student fees; and since I was living as a woman, success was dependent on an easily recognizable feminine attribution. So I did not take the task of grooming lightly. And thrown into this troublesome mixture was the fact that I had no training in the basics of womanly dress, little money to experiment, and not much room for failure, which might well have meant assault in addition to losing my job.

Initially, I had no close female friends to whom I could turn for help. Two months after I began living as Claudine, my psychologist (a man) mentioned that I was wearing too much mascara, and this marked my first advice on tasteful feminine attire. But my greatest concern was how to avoid an excessive opportunity cost in dressing: i.e., if one spends a given amount of time on Project A, it is contingent that one forfeits the opportunity to use that interval for Projects B, C, and D. I wanted to make sure that I didn't spend so much time being sexually packaged that I missed out on being educated, productive, and intelligent, which I never learned to separate from being a woman. This remains an ongoing concern.[32]

5. I discovered that as a woman, even though I was still three-dimensional in body, I was almost non-existent to men if I didn't dress attractively – and sometimes to women as well. As an attributed man, I was frequently pushed into role conformity; as a woman, I was ignored into it. To some degree, my status as an observably sexual creature established my status as a person,

and failure to respond appropriately when prompted would often result in criticism. For example, at the age of twenty-two, I politely said, "No thanks," when a man asked me to spend a weekend with him on Catalina Island. He responded with a concerned, "I don't care about homosexual guys one way or the other, but a lesbian is a waste of womanhood, and that really hurts me." Waste for whom? (Would I have accepted this line if I had been through genital surgery?) Another man wanted to spend the night with me after our first date. I refused his several requests. He called one week later and blurted angrily, "Well, now that you're over your period, maybe you'll sleep with me." Not only does attributed gender beget attributed sex, but apparently "attributed fertility." The myriad of assumptions by these men about my reasons for not wanting to have sex came as a shock to a person who a short time before had never been perceived as female, let alone as a woman "suffering" menstruation or lesbianism.

6. Women behave differently around men. I noticed that if I were with a group of women in the college cafeteria, drinking coffee, chatting, or discussing course assignments, and a man approached, conversational behavior changed dramatically. Women would smile more, talk less seriously, change vocal cadence to a more child-like pattern, and would not debate matters as formally with a man as they would with women. When I commented about this to one of my friends who seemed less affected, she agreed that it happened and added that I, too, reacted noticeably to the presence of a man. "You don't talk differently," she commented, "but you sure sit a lot straighter." She was right, and I was embarrassed. I showed deference to "maleness" without knowing much about the person who held the position.

7. Men and women kept telling me to smile, sometimes assuring me that everything would then be OK or that I'd "look pretty." Today, I try to smile only when I feel like it, but I smile much more than I ever did as a man. I can't tell if this is because I'm less miserable or because of the strong positive reinforcement. I smile as a form of greeting, much like saying, "Hello."

The social expectations that followed a new attributed gender were startling, but so was my conscious and unconscious willingness to be led by them. Being trapped in the wrong body is one kind of prison; trapped in the right body is another.

One woman, a 70-year-old MTF who underwent sex reassignment at the age of 68, related the following story:

> After I had surgery, I patently refused to wear slacks for a long while. My wife would often comment, especially when the weather was cold, that I might be more comfortable in trousers, but my response was something like, "I spent a lifetime

to get to a point where I can wear dresses, and I'm not about to climb back into pants." Perhaps a year after surgery, I decided to work in the garden and put on a pair of slacks with a blouse so that I could dig around comfortably. My wife noticed, commented that I looked great, and said, "Now you look like one of us!"[33]

I have known this woman for two years, and visited with her on perhaps fifteen occasions, and I have yet to see her in anything but a dress. Her clothes are generally elegant and feminine, with soft pastel colors, and she wears limited makeup, suitable jewelry, and the whole presentation seems appropriate for her age. Her manners are likewise delicate, except that she becomes agitated in describing incidents where she was treated "as generally incompetent." But even if we assume that the genders of this particular transsexual and her "wife" are inherently feminine, culture still shapes and/or distorts personality, and a feminine gender raised in a male body will not have the same psychology as one reared as a girl from birth. As the transsexual enters the new gender role, she gradually masters the expressions of identity that were previously forbidden. She learns, in the words of an observant wife, "to look like one of us." And while the coercive aspects of role cannot transpose core gender, they can certainly alter expression.

Part of the reassignment task is to become comfortable with one's gender and its relationship to role – to "feel like one of us" – so that the common sense of wearing pants in winter isn't overruled by the compulsion of new-found freedom. Natural females have a lifetime to test the rules against common sense and identity; MTFs must test over a shorter space with a contentious body. I speak knowingly when I say that gender comfort can be strained.

Parts of Identity

I interviewed a woman and her spouse of forty years at their home in Southern California. The wife referred to her sex-changed spouse with the feminine pronoun, saying, "Oh, she'd like to spend more money on clothes sometimes," or bragging, "She's very handy around the house and can fix anything." And as we finished the formal interview, I was invited into a study to see earlier photographs of this subject, prior to the sex change. There were several snapshots. The wife pointed to one of a boy, perhaps thirteen years old, and reported happily, "Here's one when she was younger."[34]

With regard to pronoun reference, it appears that present attributed gender – how the person is perceived and *known* – is generally dominant over past attribution (the photograph representing the subject in 1939), even with a person who has known the individual intimately before and after the sex change. However, while the spouse used feminine pronouns predominantly during my two-hour visit to refer to her reassigned partner, the subject indicates that pronouns are often mixed. The wife uses "she" most of the time.

This contradicts most of my experiences regarding present attribution by childhood friends that I discussed in Chapter 1. For present attribution to override the past, it appears that the attributor must interact frequently with the sex-changed person and have a strong motivation for inverting perception. Those individuals who persistently used "correct" referential pronouns were usually spouses, parents, children, or siblings who wanted to maintain their relationships with the transsexual. Without regular contact with the new attributed gender and the willingness to receive it, past attribution will be dominant. My own relatives still refer to me as "he." Many parents of transsexuals said that it was difficult to think of their child in the "new gender," and one mother commented, "I still occasionally slip and call my daughter 'he.'"[35]

The pronoun referent is connected to present attributed gender, but past attribution generally requires the corresponding pronoun, even from the transsexual. One FTM brought many photographs from childhood and adolescence. He is now perceived as a man, but I pointed to his kindergarten photo and asked: "If you could talk to that girl in the photograph, now, what would you tell her?" His reply: "Brace yourself! . . . but see, I think I already knew back then . . . I don't know what I could tell her that she kind of didn't already know at the time."[36]

And I talked with a sympathetic and concerned father of a male-to-female transsexual, and he consistently used feminine pronouns to refer to his after-transition daughter, but masculine pronouns to refer to his pre-transition son. I listened to him carefully for forty minutes and did not detect any mismatch, even though daughter and son are the same person. The father related:

I had three sons. I always knew this one was somehow different. I couldn't decipher exactly how, but he was not as macho or aggressive or something as the others. This was obvious from the get-go, yet I could never figure out what the problem was until he told me he wanted a sex change.

Before he started living as a woman, he was always extremely introverted, and you could hardly get him to talk at the family gatherings. Sometimes he would play the guitar and sing, but that was about it. Now, after she's been living as a woman for six months, you can't get her to shut up. She not only has overcome her introverted nature, she has become quite a personality. It's amazing.

So I see lots of improvement, but I want to be sure she's doing the right thing. I worry that maybe she won't find a good career. Maybe she'll never find a husband. There's prejudice against transsexuals.[37]

It also appears that one cannot hold two attributed genders for the same person at the same time. I offer the following account of an incident that occurred in Spring 1975, when I was twenty-one years old, ten months after I had changed my social status.

I was shopping for clothes at a department store in Pomona, California. Unbeknownst to me, my aunt, who had never seen me in feminine presentation, and my maternal grandmother, who had, were also in the store. They noticed me first. I saw them and approached. The conversation, which was cordial, pleasant, and laced with an Alabama accent, went something like this (I am referred to as "Tony," and family members still use that name):

Claudine:	Hi, Maw-maw! Hi, Marlene!
Grandma:	Hi. Marlene was jus' askin me if that was you. She weren't sure at first. But I told her course it was.
Aunt Marlene:	Hi, Tony! Well, I sure didn't know that was you. But I said to her, I said right off, "That girl looks like E! She sure does look like E!" [*Referring to my mother.*] And then I says, "Is that Tony? Is that him?"
Grandma:	[*Laughs*] That's right. That's how it happened. She didn't know you, but you look like E all right. There's no mistaken. But she didn't know you. Had to ask. She said, "That girl over there, she looks like E."
Aunt Marlene:	[*Laughs; looks at my grandmother*] Yes, ma'am. He sure does. Looks like her clear.

It was startling to hear my aunt, who had seen me often from birth until a year before I changed my name, refer to me as a girl who looked like my mother, using "she," and ten seconds later switch to the masculine pronoun in restating that proposition. The usage flip was brought on by (1) my aunt's immediate attribution of "woman" to the familiar-looking stranger and (2) the instantaneous change when she realized that "the girl" was her nephew. When Auntie understood that there were not two people involved, the lifetime masculine attribution for Tony claimed precedence over the initial feminine attribution of the stranger. Further, the feminine attribution prevented her from otherwise recognizing her nephew, despite the fact that she had known me for twenty years and watched me grow from infancy to early adulthood. This was surprising because I did not have cosmetic surgery to alter my features, I was not wearing noticeable makeup, and my clothes were androgynous – I believe I wore jeans and a turtle-neck sweater, although my hair was six to eight inches longer. And my aunt was aware of the reassignment; from what I've heard, my family talked of little else.

Similarly, while viewing childhood photographs of a female-to-male transsexual, I found it difficult to grasp emotionally that the grammar school or high school pictures were earlier representations of the 34-year-old man sitting in my living room. As I tried to guess which "little girl" was "him," I would invariably use the feminine pronoun, and when screening subsequent photos, I would speculate on the basis of which picture looked most like the preceding shot, instead of trying to match the present man to past images – I could never make a connection. Since I had not known this person as a woman, and since I could not now visualize him as anything but male, I basically saw two different individuals, and would refer to the photos by one set of pronouns and the man by another. This contrasts with the spouse who referred to her MTF partner's masculine childhood photos as "her."

An excerpt from my interview with the above-referenced FTM reads:

Alex: But I do have some photos that I thought would be interesting to you. I don't think . . . actually, a lot of this stuff probably isn't anything.

Claudine: Oh, it would be very interesting to me. Is it while you were growing up?

Alex: Yeah. Yeah.

Claudine: Oh, I think that's terrific.

Alex: Well, see, I don't know if those are in order though . . .

Claudine: Do they need to be?

Alex: Well, let's see . . . Want to work backwards or work forwards?

Claudine: Oh, forwards. Start with the youngest.

Alex: [*He shows me a collection of school class photos.*] OK, there's kindergarten. And that's me.

Claudine: Unbelievable, but I'll take your word for it. Was this in, I believe you said Illinois?

Alex: Fort Wayne, Indiana.

Claudine: . . . OK.

Alex: That's second grade.

Claudine: Where did you go? There?

Alex: No. Actually, second grade was [*pauses*] . . .

Claudine: [*Laughs*] Oh, you cut your hair.

Alex: [*Laughs*] I was expressing myself a little bit more. Yeah. So I kind of went through periods of back and forth.

Claudine: So, already in second grade you were aware of something.

Alex: Yeah. Third grade. Mom was winning the battle in third grade. [*Laughter*]

Claudine: Boy, that is a group. Looks like my photos. Except I would have been "him."

Alex: [*Laughs*] Yeah, just the opposite.

. . .

Claudine: [*Back to the photos.*] So I assume this is you now.

Alex: Yes, that's me. Yep.

Claudine: And what grade was this? Fifth?

Alex: Fifth. And then sixth. That one might be a little tougher.

Claudine: [*Guessing*] Are you wearing glasses?

Alex: No.

Claudine: Well, then I've lost you again, unless it's her.

Alex: Yep. That's it.

Claudine: Boy, you did change your hairstyles.

Alex: Yeah. I always wanted it short. Mom always wanted it long. We battled back and forth.

Claudine: I had the same battle.

Alex: [Laughter] Yeah. In reverse . . . And these are a little more. Actually, this is, I think this is ninth or tenth grade. But that's a little more of how I really looked. After I started, uh. This was a year after moving out to California, and actually that was a picture taken for a church directory, and that was my senior picture. The one and only time I ever had a perm and clipped, er, plucked my eyebrows, so – I had makeup on that day. [*Laughs.*] Kind of scary.

Claudine: Well. It sure is a difference. It's, I mean, you look at that [photo] and you'd say, "Oh, there's a very attractive, happy, person – woman." I mean, that's what you would think.

Alex: Uh-huh [*laughs awkwardly*].

It is disturbing that I cannot "attribute" the photos of a young girl to the 36-year-old man whom I have come to know during my work on this book. It seems important to grasp that this person has a whole life, even if it is partitioned by a change in attributed gender. Sometimes I must remind even myself that life did not begin when I became a recognizable woman. To disregard existence before reassignment and to consider the "little girl" as independent from the "man" diminishes perception. This FTM's gender may have been consistently masculine throughout childhood and adolescence – his proclamation and my belief – but over half of his life was spent as an attributed "girl/woman."

It is self-evident that a femininely gendered female will receive different instruction from a femininely gendered male. Gender-role training is based on sex, and if sex is ambiguous it cannot begin until after "final" assignment;

and identity, itself, is irrelevant in the implementation of training. Nor will gender role be modified for the ambiguously sexed child after final assignment: i.e., a genetic female born with a masculinizing syndrome who is assigned and reared as a boy will not receive mitigated training – the role will be the same as for a genetic male. What is not self-evident is how much of gender identity is determined prenatally and how much is learned after our first-day sex announcement, from which designation is derived the absolute presumption of boy or girl.

It appears that in some individuals gender is malleable enough to be influenced or redirected by sex reassignment in infancy, though an imposed reassignment is generally not recommended after the age of 18 months.[38] However, we also know that "once the core gender identity has differentiated, a change of sexual status will not automatically be followed by a corresponding change in gender identity."[39] And there is the transsexual population who are born with normal male or female anatomies, receive "appropriate" training, but do not develop concordant genders.

Gender identity may vary by degree and *perhaps* solidify in early childhood, but on the basis of my own case history, those of over a hundred transsexuals I've talked with and the several dozen I've read about, I warrant that gender is as physical as a heartbeat. We need only learn to measure its pulse. Public expression and private experience are derivatives of physiology and culture. The precise relationships will undoubtedly confound investigators for many years, but gender identity is more than a concept, it is an indelible constituent of the mind.

4

Sexualities and Genders

Ancillary Attributions

If gender identity is the private experience of gender role, then for transsexuals genital surgery is an improvement in that experience. The degree of improvement will vary from individual to individual, just as, predictably, surgery on non-transsexuals would be disturbing to varying degrees.

Transsexuals often reform genitalia in their efforts to adapt body to gender. There are different procedures for the construction of a vagina in MTFs or a penis in FTMs, which I will discuss and/or allow other transsexuals to discuss in quotation. But in addition to the physical changes of sex-reassignment surgery, there are some interesting social and psychological considerations.

John Money writes:

> in general usage, homosexuality is not defined on the basis of chromosomal sex, nor of any of the internal and concealed variables of sex. Instead, it is defined on the basis of the external sexual anatomy and the sexual characteristics of the body in general. Two people are identified as having a homosexual encounter or relationship provided their external sex organs are anatomically of the same sex, regardless of how different they may be in secondary sexual characteristics.[1]

This gives rise to a series of questions and propositions, because in my experience it does not ring completely true; however, with my background, I'm not sure that it would be possible to construct a statement about homo-sexuality or heterosexuality that would strike me as "completely" true.

First, Money is referring to the case history of a genetic female (XX) who was born with the adrenogenital syndrome, which induced masculinization of the external genitalia. In this case, the genetically female baby had a penis and empty scrotum, yet also ovaries and internal female reproductive organs. It was assigned and reared as a boy, grew into a man, and married a genetic female. In reference to the couple, Money asks, "Are he and his wife both lesbians?" Based on the above-cited criteria, he answers "No."[2] I agree, though I question the apparent deductive simplicity. It doesn't seem that genital morphology is *the* defining aspect of "homosexual" or "heterosexual," but is rather one attribute of a homosexual or heterosexual encounter. Even Money speaks of "characteristics of the body in general" as a consideration.

I arrive at this conclusion simply because I have lived a life where identical sexual behavior on the part of the same person with the same genital morphology has been deemed heterosexual and appropriate at one time and homosexual and inappropriate at another. The varying states of my body and attributed gender in which these evaluations took place were: living as a man until the age of twenty, living as a woman with male genitalia until the age of thirty-seven, and then living as a woman with female genitalia until my present age of forty-three; and, of course, throughout all this my genetic karyotype has remained the same. And the rendezvous were not clinical demonstrations for sociologists, therapists, or psychologists; they were everyday encounters with the general public – men and women, friends, family, and suitors. It is and has been a day-to-day existence under the constraints of attributed gender that has resulted in approval or disapproval of behavior and, in many instances, defined that behavior.

My arguments focus on awareness that attributed gender begets attributed sex – I discuss this in Chapter 1, citing Holly Devor's *Gender Blending*. And I question whether, in general social evaluations, attributed gender will likewise beget "attributed heterosexuality" and/or "attributed homo-sexuality." This is more than just wordplay, and I state flatly that one can encounter hostility for attributed homosexuality that by Money's genital definition may not be homosexual behavior, and one can be pressured to conform to attributed heterosexuality that would directly counter the genital criterion. (There was a recent widely reported case of "gay bashing" in Laguna Beach, California. Ironically, the victim was heterosexual, but was perceived as gay by the basher.)

Attributed Sexuality

Let me recount some experiences that will partially clarify the confusion I have seen and lived. At the age of twenty, I altered my attributed gender through change of clothes and manner, and gradual transformation of secondary sex characteristics. A feminine gender was imputed to me by strangers, by co-workers, fellow students, men who asked me out, and women who suggested that I date those men. During my first few months as a woman, I did not date; in fact, I did not have much social life at any level. I was much too frightened by a contemplated negative response from a potential suitor. But immediately after attributed gender changed, so did expectations from those around me as to what was considered acceptable romantic behavior. To my surprise, men would ask me out on a date; when I refused once, they would often ask again; usually about the third time, most would insist that I tell them why I would not see them socially. Sometimes their suspicion was stated without equivocation, and they would demand, "Are you a lesbian?" or, more typical of 1974, "Are you queer? a faggot? some kind o' dyke?" Sometimes men wouldn't even inquire about whether I were homosexual, but would make that assumption and ask "How long have you been a lesbian?", usually proclaiming that being with a man, particularly themselves, would help me overcome this condition. Female friends at school or at work would likewise encourage me to date men, insisting, "Claudine, I think going out with [Anyman] would be good for you," or, "A woman needs a man once in a while," and, "You're crazy if you turn him down." All of this without knowing anything about my genitalia or transsexuality, and on the basis instead of assumptions derived from attributed gender and a perceived incongruous behavior. (Much of this happened during my first quarter at college as Claudine, before people discovered I was transsexual; several months later, when it seemed that ten thousand students suddenly knew about me, I found new pressures on campus.) And these comments were not because of any "tomboyishness" on my part that I was aware of; indeed, I was compulsively "feminine" during the first few months because I was terrified of failing to pass as a woman. After I had said "no" to one man four times, he called me "a prude," and since I'd never heard the word, and since it was obviously no compliment from a 1974-free-love *hombre*, I looked up the meaning to find out what he had called me. I thought I was being "ladylike."

These comments were elicited because of *absence* of behavior that was considered appropriate for my attributed gender. I should add that my romantic posture immediately prior to my changed social identity was the same, i.e., I abstained from close personal relationships or dating. And while I was in the last months of living as a man, not one male ever accused me of being a lesbian because I wouldn't date him, nor did any woman ever suggest I should go out with Mr Right because it would be good for me. Suspicion arose when I was perceived as a woman who said "No" too often.

During this time – after I changed attributed gender and when I finally risked dating – my family's reactions were quite different. Mother and Father did not approve of my dating men, but condoned, and still do, my emotional and sexual involvement with women. As I have mentioned, my attributed gender did not change for my parents, even if it did change with everyone else around me. Nor did social prescription or prohibition seem related to awareness of my genitalia. Almost all the men and women who knew me as Claudine but eventually discovered that I had a penis reacted as if the discovery were irrelevant – I should engage in "heterosexual" behavior for a woman, i.e., date men, *display an interest* in such behavior, and not have romantic attachments to "other women." The power of attributed gender usually overwhelms the matter of genitalia.

Fragmented Attributions and Prescriptions

It was a rare and distressing predicament to find general society criticizing me for not dating men and also discouraging sexual attachments to women, which was my own proscription as well, yet to find family members urging or demanding that I form a relationship with a woman and being unhappy about even the suggestion of intimate relationships with men. Nor can this be ascribed to my family's knowledge of primary sex characteristics, since it is obvious, both before and after genital surgery, that Mother and Father still approve of my relationship with my female lover. This, again, is based on their evaluation of gender. On the other hand, even when they make efforts to approve, and even after they had cordially accepted my one live-in male lover fifteen years ago, my parents cannot hide the fact that they consider my relationships with men to be homosexual (bad) and my relationships with women to be heterosexual (good). The rest of the world works in reverse.

And there was an encounter in 1977 with a man I knew from high school. We bumped into each other in the lobby of a movie theater in Claremont, California. I was wearing a tight-fitting, red turtle-neck sweater with dress slacks. The man had seen me before and was always cordial, but this time he stared wide-eyed at my upper torso and said: "Claudine, wow! You look goooood!" He appeared to be speaking to my breasts, which was disconcerting, and then gestured with an easy, locker-room manner. "You must really enjoy playing with those." As nearly as I could figure, he thought that I was a man who had gained a female body so I could have a heterosexual affair with myself. This was supposed to be complimentary, I think.

But how does gender itself play into my homosexual versus heterosexual deliberations?

Money continues, hypothetically, and asserts,

The 46,XX gonadal female with a penis and empty scrotum assigned and reared as a boy would be classified as homosexual if he had an affair with another person with a penis. However, if he were to do something so far unheard of, namely to undergo surgical sex reassignment and then continue the affair with the same lover, then the relationship would be redefined as heterosexual.[3]

73

My questions: Defined by whom? unheard of by whom? and redefined by whom? As I will illustrate below, the situation of sex-change-and-same-lover does occur with transsexuals.

Here, again, a hypothetical change in primary sex characteristics, with all other factors remaining the same, would purportedly transfigure a sexual relationship from homosexual to heterosexual. Yet the attributed gender of the gonadal female assigned and reared as a boy would still be masculine, along with attributed sex, and the relationship would still be universally classified as homosexual by non-clinical observers. And if two men are seen walking hand-in-hand or kissing in certain urban neighborhoods in Southern California, the fact that one man may have a vagina and the other a penis will carry no determinative function in the bashing to follow.

And there is the further convolution of "gender identity" to be thrown into the mixture regarding "attributed homosexuality." As a transsexual, I consider that I can be logically classified as heterosexual or homosexual no matter what type of sexual relationship I find. By genetics (XY), despite the fact that I have secondary female characteristics and a vagina, I could arguably be a homosexual man if I date a man, or a heterosexual man if I date a woman; by hormones, I would be considered homosexual with a woman; by genitalia, heterosexual with a man; by attributed gender, lesbian if I love a woman; by birth certificate, I am a husband if I marry a female. But despite an array of viable deductions arising from a distinct pageantry, there is no confusion to me: "I am a female, heterosexual woman in a lesbian relationship." Clarity has surfaced through an understanding of gender and its relationship to body.

Part of my certainty comes from my understanding of gender as a physical element of identity. I knew that I was a girl/woman even when there were no outward physical signs to support the belief, and I challenged my own judgment many times on that basis – ultimately to no avail. The reality of gender cannot be excluded from definitions of heterosexuality or homosexuality. This may be irrelevant for 99.995 per cent of the population, because sex and gender commonly match; but in those cases where they don't, the distinction is important. Body morphology does not exclusively define homosexuality or heterosexuality. Attributed gender and gender identity are mandatory sub-clauses. The self-image of each of the principals in a relationship, their reciprocal attributions, the psychological bases of their erotic responses, and third-party perceptions must be considered.

Money, generally a knowledgeable, sympathetic, and credible authority on gender differentiation and "cross-coding," states:

Social conformity to the cultural criterion of femininity (or, vice versa, masculinity) does not, per se, override the genital criterion of homosexuality. To illustrate, in the case of a morphologically normal male who is a female impersonator: no matter how ladylike the appearance, or how hormonally feminized the body, the impersonator who is a lady with a penis is still regarded morally and legally as a homosexual (or perhaps as a preoperative transsexual) if she has a sexual partner who also has a penis.[4]

However, even though social conformity to cultural models may not override the genital criterion of homosexuality, it is more important to recognize that there are different criteria, neither necessarily overriding the other, and neither providing an immutable definition of homosexuality or heterosexuality. The whole gender/attributed-gender package must be considered – and I will soon add the matter of genitalia, which can enhance or inhibit gender expression depending on the associated expectations and private experience of gender role. For example, one pre-operative MTF said that she often has sexual encounters with heterosexual men who do not know that she is transsexual. In some encounters she performed oral sex for her partner, without herself getting undressed or exposing her genitalia. I contend that one could not define the man's sexual behavior as homosexual simply because he allowed an "attributed female" to perform fellatio, even though his partner likewise had a penis. One could argue that the event was homosexual for one party and heterosexual for the other (an interesting concept), but in this particular instance I assert that it was heterosexual for both and would universally be classified as heterosexual by any "viewer" who did not know that the woman's attributed sex did not actually correspond with her genitalia.

Categories of Sexuality – The Love Test

Money also refers to the "Skyscraper Test," which is essentially putting an individual into the hypothetical situation of either performing a sexual act against his or her nature or alternatively jumping off a building. He writes:

This Skyscraper Test, by dramatizing the difference between act and status, points to the criterion of falling in love as the definitive criterion of homosexual, heterosexual, and bisexual status. A person with a homosexual status is one who has the potential to fall in love only with someone who has the same body sex – the same genital and body morphology – as the self. For the heterosexual, the morphology must be that of a person of the other sex. For the bisexual it may be either.[5]

The "falling in love" test for homosexuality or heterosexuality, for a variety of reasons that I will discuss, seems a more encompassing and accurate definition; yet, at the same time, it contradicts Money's assertion that the genital-to-genital criterion is the determining factor. Falling in love or genital contact cannot each simultaneously be the definitive measure. But Money, through his work at The Johns Hopkins Hospital and School of Medicine, has encountered and contemplated many variations of psychological and physical sexuality, and there is a connection between the love test and genitalia. This makes sense even if neither measure wholly dominates the other or if one relates to "status" and the other to "the act." That connection is gender identity.

Sexualities – The Gender Test

It seems impossible to classify homosexuality or heterosexuality without considering core identity, even bearing in mind that verification of gender in transsexuals appears to be the "real-life test" to confirm that the individual can adapt to the new role. If we contemplate variables such as (1) *gender identity*: Does the individual define himself or herself as a man or woman? (2) *attributed gender and its corresponding attributed sex*: Is the individual readily accepted by strangers, friends, co-workers, and possibly family as a man or woman? and (3) *sexual or erotic orientation*: Is the individual capable of falling in love with a man or woman (or either)? – then we can develop more accommodating definitions of homosexuality, heterosexuality, or bisexuality as they relate to transsexuals or anybody else. Whether or not we need such definitions is another question; but for the purpose of under-standing how a transsexual is likely to be perceived socially, I offer these contemplations, though I will spare the reader the additional manifestations of an FTM who establishes a heterosexual relationship with an MTF.

The answer to the equation 2 + 2 is 4. It is readily accepted as 4. But if we consider that homosexuality or heterosexuality is as easily understood as "4", there remain the factors of the equation that produces it. They may be 2 + 2; 2 x 2; 1 + 3; 8 divided by 2; or gender identity + attributed gender + genital morphology + falling in love + object of love = heterosexual man. One cannot know the answer until one knows the variables; and concerning human sexuality, the variables are intricate.

I include "gender vs. gender" in the determination of homosexuality or heterosexuality, instead of the "genital" or "love" criterion alone, because I view genitalia, love, secondary characteristics, attributed gender, and gender identity as interactionally dependent. Nor do I see definitions of homosexuality or heterosexuality as necessary for prescription, but as elements of social and self-understanding. If society is to overcome prejudices against "deviant" sexual behavior – behavior which may not be deviant in any sense other than that of being a violation of predominantly accepted gender-role maxims – it seems worthwhile to look at some of the associated "attributions" brought about by a change in attributed gender. While gender identity and its fabrics of love and erotic object may remain constant, a new attributed gender and reconstructed genitalia bring many changes.

Reconstructed Sexualities

I met one "heterosexual" couple who had remained together for five years and described shifting perceptions of their relationship – first as a homosexual couple (two men) and later as a heterosexual couple, after one partner changed her attributed gender and morphological sex. They commented that they were once asked to leave a gay bar for "being disruptively straight," that some of their gay friends ultimately rejected them because they "became heterosexual," and the community at large now perceives them as a "normal" couple and often expects them to have similar prejudices against aberrant behaviors/statuses to those that are harbored by many of their new heterosexual, middle-class neighbors. The same two individuals in a single relationship are now subjected to the same gender-role expectations of husband and wife that were once prohibited them as two attributed gay male lovers. Attached to the many preconceptions associated with attributed gender are correlative assumptions about homosexuality or heterosexuality. The wife's summary comment was, "I don't think there is such a thing as homosexual or heterosexual. My husband is the same person. I am the same person. But everybody sees us differently now. It's very strange."[6] This couple suddenly became respectable through a change in attributed gender. The fact that it came as a surprise does not alter the reality of their new attributions – as individuals and as a couple. Not only did the wife not have the attribution of "woman" prior to reassignment, but there was no investiture with the title of "husband" or "wife" for either member of the couple, even between themselves, before her change in attributed gender.

Professor Jacob Hale comments on the shifting perceptions after he changed into a "man":

> behavioral pressures changed dramatically in heterosexual settings – I do not know those interactional dynamics and "rules" very well, so often feel I do not know how to behave "appropriately" and thus feel awkward; however, I am not sure I

really want to know, and am sure that I don't want to engage in appropriate heterosexual behaviors.[7]

Another female-to-male subject, when asked about personal relationships after changing his attributed gender, stated:

I have no clue . . . I guess I've been so busy, I've just kind of buried myself in my work and have had absolutely no social life. Now, I'm ready for a social life again . . . I see everything at a real developmental level, and think that we have to go through certain phases before we can go on if we're really going to mature into adults, even though we're already adults . . . I feel like I started out as an infant six years ago and am still growing up . . . I'm getting back into that early adulthood type thing where I'm ready for a relationship now. But *I've never been a straight guy in our society before*. I've never had to deal with women in this sort of sense. And it's all very new to me, and it's very intimidating . . . Plus the complications of my anatomy . . . I can't just jump into things.[8]

This man, who is unambiguously masculine in appearance, has secondarily changed his relationship with society from that of a "major bull dyke" to that of a heterosexual man. And this was not brought about by a change in dress or manner, for by the subject's own proclamations he had been wearing men's clothes for many years prior to reassignment and had been dating women as well. What changed was attributed gender. In this man's life, external behavioral expressions have remained the same. He continues to wear men's clothes and to date women. But once he took male hormones, developed masculine secondary sex characteristics, and had his breasts surgically removed, the interactional perceptions were altered. He talked about life before and after:

I'd always dressed masculine . . . I was already as masculine as I could be in our society, and actually it was a big relief when I transitioned, because I was so kind of unusual looking that I would remember I'd walk into a room or walk into a restaurant and I'd turn heads, because I was – whatever . . . And once I transitioned, it was like, quiet. [*Whispers the word.*] All of a sudden, I didn't turn heads any more, I fit in, and it was so much more relaxing and comfortable.[9]

By inverting attributed gender, the subject became "average" to his fellow citizens, which among transsexuals is a genuinely treasured experience. Instead of having people stare at him because he was perceived as a woman acting and looking like a man, he became a "typical guy," hardly worth a second glance from an uninterested stranger. Without altering comportment, he lost the status of a lesbian and was transformed into a heterosexual male in the eyes of others. The fact that this man has a vagina is irrelevant in the trick of attributed gender. But does it remain extraneous when he contemplates a sexual relationship with a woman? or when a woman contemplates a relationship with him? Does the man, at the figurative stroke of midnight, become a lesbian again?

One pre-op MTF, who remains in a supportive, close relationship with her former wife, writes: "I would never [have] thought of myself [as] someone having a problem being perceived as lesbian, and the resulting social pressure angers me more than the . . . pressure against making a gender role change."[10] She also mentions that her wife "does not experience the difficulty in being perceived as a lesbian that I do."[11] Can a male-to-female transsexual who remains in love with her wife explain convincingly to third parties that she's not really a lesbian? Is she a lesbian for that matter? or a heterosexual man? What about the wife? These questions may be debated on many levels, but it is clear that this transsexual is perceived as a lesbian and does not like it.

During one of my interviews, an FTM also mentioned his dislike of the lesbian attribution:

Mister: For instance, a butch lesbian, before my transition, made me very uncomfortable, because that's what people took me as – and that made me very uncomfortable. That was not who I was or who I wanted to be perceived as.

. . .

Claudine: Do you consider yourself a heterosexual male?
Mister: Yes. Completely.[12]

Such quibbling may seem inconsequential, but it can have a sobering effect on those who must face it in earnest. It is difficult for a man to tell a woman that he has no penis, especially if he is falling in love with her; it is difficult for the woman to hear it. What seems to enable "love" to overcome the genital contradiction is the absolute certainty that attributed gender *is* gender. Thus, the importance of establishing an unambiguous presentation through hormone therapy and/or reconstructive surgery weighs heavily. Solid attribution increases the chance that a potential lover will recognize the man belonging to the body and respond erotically, gender to gender, without doubting the nature of the encounter. And this has been my experience as an attributed woman, whether I had a male or female lover, and whether or not I had had genital surgery.

For example, I had a brief affair in 1977. The man was heterosexual, did not know that I was transsexual when we met, and remained attracted to me after I told him. We had been dating about three months when he complained that I didn't spend enough time with him and suggested, "I want you out of school. It's a waste, because you'll just end up as a housewife anyway." I had already been annoyed by his sexist comments, and retaliated "It's people like you who make me hate being a woman." I naively expected an apology, but he laughed. It was a kind of laugh I had never heard before, sinister and amused, and it underscored his response: "I got a newsflash for you, Cutie. You're a woman, like it or not. Better get used to it." His awareness that I had a penis and had lived as a man, which he considered the anomalous experience, did not change his perception that I was securely bound to role. My attributed gender discounted other factors. It is also apparent that three years of a new identity was affecting me.

FTMs generally have the advantage over MTFs in attribution because of the profound changes brought on by testosterone. The only visible clue that these men were born female is their height, often ranging from 5'2" to 5'7". Otherwise, I found no way to guess that the clothed subjects were not natural males, and it is easy to recognize and believe in gender identity when attributed gender is so compelling. Ironically, the attributional advantage gained by FTMs through supplemental testosterone is comparable to the disadvantage that MTFs receive through natural adolescence. But attributed gender affects attributed homosexuality, attributed heterosexuality, and many non-consensual role assumptions, which may or may not be in harmony with the wishes of the transsexual. New social rules must be confronted.

Again, because gender is essentially invisible except as represented through the body, and because gender role is anticipated on the basis of attribution, it is effectively impossible to relate to a feminine gender that is wrapped by a male physiology, or vice versa. When I initially told psychologists and close friends that I was transsexual – in my words, "a woman in a man's body" – and after psychological testing had preliminarily sustained my evaluation, these individuals still could not relate to me as "Claudine" when what they saw was a male. It is likewise impossible for me to relate emotionally to a man whom I see as a female, even when I try to. If I stop for a moment consciously thinking of the person's gender, I react to the body. As physiology begins to change, so does my perception of the inner person. When I meet a transsexual who has already been through sex reassignment, I generally find it impossible to visualize the person's having lived in the opposite role.

The immutability of attributed gender is not subject to my own sympathies with or awareness of the individual's gender identity. I know the struggle, and I have apologized on several occasions for using a feminine pronoun to refer to a female who is going through sex reassignment, assuring "him" that my unconscious attribution will soon catch up with his proclaimed identity. The transsexual understands this, too. One transitioning FTM, whom I frequently called "she," responded to my apology with, "Don't worry. It hurts, but I know you're not doing it intentionally."[13] I felt bad but could not force my desired pronoun use. After this individual had taken male hormones for six months, I started using masculine references without effort; after 18 months, I wondered how I could ever have "seen" a woman. But not only has the body rearranged its physical expressions, but gender has intensified its behavioral expressions; or perhaps I simply allow myself to see the countenance more clearly. According to many FTMs, behavior itself changes because of (1) the psychological effects of testosterone and (2) their growing freedom to "be the man I always was."

Relative Values of Surgery

The bodies of female-to-male transsexuals are so effectively altered by hormone therapy that they are supremely confident in their attributions as men. This contrasts with many MTFs, who never escape the fear of being read. And the powerful change in attributed gender for FTMs seems to strengthen similarly their self-concepts. They have an XX karyotype, and they may have been married as women (rare) or carried their own pregnancies (very rare); and they may still have a uterus, ovaries, and vagina. But past or current physical condition does not seem to undermine post-transition self-attribution. For example, one man unapologetically discussed the "femaleness" of his body without any indication of feeling less masculine:

Claudine: You said it took nine months after you started taking hormones before you noticed physical changes?

Alex: Six months before I started noticing. Nine months when it became obvious to other people.

Claudine: What were the first changes you noticed?

Alex: The voice. The voice. That's about it, really. The facial hair. I had been working out before that, so I'd always been pretty built up. Actually, I haven't worked out in a long time, and I'm stronger now than even when I was working out five times a week. But, um, I don't know. I had a lot of change in my face. I don't know if it was just the muscles or the cartilage. But all my glasses, I had to replace my glasses a number of times because it was digging into the side of my head. My face really widened. My nose widened. The bridge of my eyebrows and face widened up. I started measuring myself and had measured my bones for the first six months to a year. And was getting like, my finger knuckles had increased a quarter of an inch, that sort of thing. So I had some major growth. My shoe size went up two sizes. So, you know, physically, but I don't think it was real obvious. That's more of just little things that I noticed. Then there was the clitoral growth and sexual arousal, which was extremely intense.

Claudine: And that came gradually . . .?

Alex: That, pretty much right off the blocks.

Claudine: OK.

Alex: Yeah, yeah. That was pretty much as soon as my period stopped, which is about a month after my, so about after my second shot, my period stopped, and I really began to notice it. Tremendous increase in my libido.

Claudine: And I can assume you were pleased about that?

Alex: Yeah, I mean, it was good, but it was also very annoying. It was extremely, to the point where I couldn't even think about other things. You know. [*Laughs.*] I mean just completely consumed. I think between just the increased libido plus the growth of the clitoris. Just engorgement in the area and everything else.

Claudine: Yeah.

Alex: It was just an extremely, almost frustrating. Cause there's just no way you could try to [*laughs*] satisfy anything. But that settled down after about a year or two.

Claudine: What doses of hormones are you taking now?

Alex: Now I'm on 1 cc 200 ml depotestosterone, which I've been on basically from the start. I believe I've got some endometriosis. I haven't had my hysterectomy yet. And had . . . some severe cramping problems about three years ago. And at that point Dr Leve increased me to one and a half, and the extra hormones did stop the pain, and the cramping and stuff.[14]

Genital surgery can improve the self-esteem of some transsexuals; yet many find that surgery is not necessary to live happily in the new role. And the decision to pursue or not to pursue genital reconstruction is based on different criteria for MTFs and FTMs. The underlying motivation may be similar (trying to match gender to a corresponding bodily representation), but the disparate surgical procedures create different realities. Vaginoplasty may be so effective that it will "fool a gynecologist," but the surgery for FTMs, which Dr Stanley Biber classifies as "still experimental,"[15] does not achieve the same cosmetic or functional results. There are more MTF surgeries than FTM, but Biber partially accounts for this when he states:

There's just as many women who want to become men as men who want to be women, but because the process isn't as satisfactory, most of them don't elect to have surgery. I might do a dozen each year. We can make everything look the way it's supposed to, but it's not really functional. I usually advise them to wait a few more years, until technology catches up.[16]

Several FTMs that I talked with expressed the same sentiments, insisting that their related genital procedures are too expensive and the results "aren't really all that great." One reported:

I had a metadioiplasty, which basically frees up the clitoris. My penis looks fine, just small. It's not big enough for penetration, but I can get an erection and it has full sensation. Since the clitoris was enlarged through hormone therapy, I don't think anybody would say, "Well, that obviously used to be a girl." But any woman I have sex with is going to notice a difference.[17]

My impression is that "quality" is only one of several reasons female-to-male transsexuals are sometimes reluctant to have surgery. Another important matter is money. Costs can be prohibitive for all transsexuals, and most insurance policies specifically exclude sex-reassignment surgery and related treatment. For FTMs the overall financial burden is three to four times that for MTFs. But I believe that more male-to-female's opt for surgery primarily because of disparate comfort levels concerning attributed gender.

In decades past, the desire for genital surgery was often considered to be an indicator of transsexualism; if the person didn't want surgery, the treating physicians might suspect the candidate wasn't a true transsexual and shouldn't receive medical support.[18] I was fortunate in 1974–5 that my psychologist, social worker, and endocrinologist never considered surgery mandatory, though all believed it should be available if I wanted it after cross-living. Gerald Leve, my endocrinologist, pointedly assured me, "No one will ever try to force you into surgery, but we will help you obtain it when the time is right." Even so, as the years increased from the time I changed my attributed gender, I did occasionally feel a gentle, concerned pressure on me to have SRS. But beyond the sphere of medical professionals directly involved with transsexuals, I found plenty of pressure, and many persons insisted at various times that I should have surgery immediately because "your mental health depends on it" or "your legal status depends on it" or "you can't possibly function as a woman" or "lawfully use a public washroom like you are now." This often came from friends or doctors (usually at the university health center) who were shaken when they found that my attributed gender did not match my sex, and who sympathetically and genuinely believed that this was not a healthy state. I agreed, of course, but was also confronted with the reality that obtaining a vagina would come at great cost and risk; I had already looked long and hard for a competent surgeon.[19]

I asked many transsexuals in 1995–7 if they encountered similar pressures to undergo surgery once they changed attributed gender. Most reported that they did not. The drive for surgery came mostly from within. I discussed this with one 69-year-old post-op MTF:

Claudine: After you started living as a woman, did you notice pressure from others to have surgery?
Ophelia: None at all.
Claudine: So the pressure came just from within you?
Ophelia: Just internal. Yeah. My own needs. As a matter of fact, I would think it would be the other way. If there was any pressure, it would probably be not to do that. Now that's an expression of – people want to preserve status quo. And those very close to you want to preserve status quo. And there's no reason why they shouldn't.[20]

Another discussion with a 51-year-old pre-op MTF transcribed as follows:

Claudine: Do you have any outside pressure to have the surgery?
Galatea: No. None. I can't think. Oh, maybe some of the TS [transsexual] friends that I have, that are post-op. I think there's a little line of demarcation.
Claudine: My guess is that when you do have it, you'll feel better and have a sense of relief, but, my feeling is still, I could have gone on as I was and not been any, probably, less happy than I am now. But any surgery is kind of – I'm glad I did it, but . . .
Galatea: Yeah. I can see that. Now that I'm thinking about it. Now that I think it's a possibility. You know, I go, "Ah, god, this would be a great thing! I won't have to look at those mirrors and avert my eyes." [*Sighs audibly.*][21]

There appears to be a greater willingness among transsexuals today to debate the necessity or desirability of surgery. In 1974 there was little argument that I can remember. It was my ultimate aim; it appeared to be the aim of every transsexual I read about; it appeared to be the prescription of doctors working with transsexuals. However, my exposure to the "transgendered" community was limited in 1974–80, so there may well have been more discussion than I know. Back then, I earnestly wanted to escape the transsexual world, not learn about it.

It is interesting that Galatea makes reference to some encouragement from "post-op" transsexuals, though other "non-ops" advise surgical candidates to reconsider their decision. But overall, it appears that transsexuals don't receive significant outside pressure to have surgery, and their internal drive often lessens after changing attributed gender. While SRS may remain a goal, surgical considerations affect its pursuit. I discussed the matter with "Alex," the above-cited 35-year-old FTM:

Alex: At this time I'm not even planning on surgery, so that's not a factor. But everything now in itself costs, you know, so I have to work two jobs. But I since moved into a house. I'm just renting a room, and uh . . .

Claudine: Yes, I worked two jobs. I remember doing that same thing to try to keep up with the medical bills. It was an enormous thing. When you say you're not planning on surgery, how do you view surgery as a matter of transition? How important is that in the scope of things?

Alex: It depends on when you ask me, you know. [*Laughs.*] I mean, if you would have asked me four years ago, it would have been a completely different answer, and that's why it – actually, for filling out a number of surveys, I'm very uncomfortable doing that, because I find that my opinions change greatly.

Claudine: I know mine have. Mine do. So what would your opinion have been say five years ago?

Alex: It would have been mandatory. Yeah. It was just a definite part of the process, and it was absolutely necessary, and it was planned.

Claudine: And as opposed to now?

Alex: As opposed to now. The more I've seen, the more I've heard about, the more I've researched, I'm not happy with what they're doing. I think it's still, for the female-to-male, I think it's very experimental. I think there's still a huge amount of risk. I think the cost is completely out of hand. It's literally, for the top of the line, between $100,000 to $150,000. Probably.

Claudine: I've heard several people say six figures for state of the art.

Alex: Yeah. If you want the radial arm flap. And that also involves major scarring of the forearm, which I'm not comfortable with, as well as scarring of the thighs, scarring of the stomach. You know, they're just taking bits and pieces from all over.

Claudine: It's a big deal.

Alex: Yeah. It's huge. And the amount of time, the amount of surgery that's involved. For something that may or may not work and may or may not do everything I want it to do, I am just not willing. So at this point, I'm more comfortable just leaving things just the way they are. I mean it's not something that I'm really comfortable with, but I've come to terms with it. So, and until they can either perfect it or the insurance will start covering it or something, I plan on just holding out.[22]

Similarly, the longer I lived as Claudine, the lower my emotional need for surgery, especially as I considered the flesh-and-blood aspects of the operation. On 6 October 1975, I wrote in my personal journal: "Had an appointment with [counselor], and we talked about my decreasing desire for surgery, which has almost become a non-desire . . . Am I wholly a woman now?" This marks a significant attitude change for a person who 18 months earlier didn't want to cross-dress until after genital reconstruction. Still, my evergreen longing to be female was never completely overcome. I eventually found an eminent surgeon and decided to go forward with the operation; but if the cost had been too high or the doctor less experienced, I would not have done it.

I believe that there are more male-to-female than female-to-male genital surgeries because: (1) the change in attributed gender for FTMs is generally more effective; (2) the aesthetic and functional quality of phalloplasty is poorer; and (3) the cost of phalloplasty is more prohibitive.

Changing attributed gender appears to be the most important element of sex reassignment. Many questionnaire respondents and interviewed subjects attest to this, and I note one further impression – the better the change in attribution, the less the need for surgery, i.e., the more easily a woman fits into her social role and the more readily she is recognized and accepted as a woman, the less motivation for surgery; likewise with a man. And since every FTM that I met appeared unquestionably male, except those who were just beginning transition, I postulate that FTMs are generally happier about their perceived masculinity than MTFs are about their femininity. And most transsexuals admit that it is more difficult for MTFs to become "inconspicuous." In the words of one Trinidad resident who has seen many of Biber's patients come and go: "They do what they can . . ., but they still look like men dressed up like women."[23] If attributed gender is in doubt, at least one can use surgery to back up self-image.

Prosthetic Comfort

But if genital reconstructive surgery may be financially out of reach or aesthetically undesirable for many FTMs, this is not a reflection on their desire for a penis. Rather, it is a reality-based consideration. And if they didn't get a factory penis, and if they can't effectively get one built, most wear some kind of prosthetic device as a substitute, often referring to the "appropriate bulge" in their pants as part of the motivation. Others admit to wearing it even when they are alone, so I am not sure this dress manifestation is exclusively for an outside audience. They want it to be perceived underneath clothing, but it also provides a degree of personal psychological comfort. One man told me he wears a prosthetic penis "almost all the time," because it makes him feel better; another wrote that he wears "prosthetic genitalia – for the realistic bulge in pants"; and a third responded that he simply uses padding in the crotch.[24]

A penis can be considered as a representation of gender, because only males have them. So if one wants to be perceived as a man, it is important to be perceived as having a penis, or at least not missing one. Even though an attributed masculine gender will give rise to an attributed penis, that is an aspect that can frequently be "verified." For female-to-male transsexuals, visual confirmation is important; it is verbalized as important. And if I judge correctly, based on the tight-fitting jeans of many natural males, it is an appropriate display for them as well. For FTMs, having a penis or the appearance of a penis is comforting.

Genital surgery reportedly can give transsexuals higher self-esteem, make them more comfortable in their role, provide "official" confirmation of gender, and help them "feel right" about their bodies; however, there are physical and psychological limitations. Questionnaire comments from MTFs and FTMs include:

[I have a good body now] . . . except it would be nice if my penis could fully react and function like the "factory equipped" variety (e.g., be able to urinate through it, become fully erect and ejaculate). [November 1995 – FTM]

. . . I felt much more confident and at ease after surgery . . . [There has been] a loss of sexual drive and/or response to genital stimulation. [October 1995 – MTF]

I only started living full-time after the S.R.S. [October 1995 – MTF]

I have simply removed a growth of the testicles which should have been ovaries and corrected the distention of my vagina. [June 1995 – MTF]

The subtle changes brought on by the years of hormones and the lack of testicles are very gratifying . . . Actually, I'm pretty happy with the way this body has turned out. I do realize now, though, that I will have to have my penis removed. It's just too jarring, and certainly seems out of place. [August 1995 – MTF]

I don't understand why I am uncomfortable with my body as a male. [July 1995 – MTF]

I pass easily and have never been questioned . . . still feel I need [further] chest revision to eliminate a couple funny "bumps" . . . still desire . . . bottom surgery. [November 1995 – FTM]

Most transsexuals recognize that even the best sex-reassignment surgery is a tradeoff. None of us ever achieves a "factory" version of femaleness or maleness after surgery like that we had before. None of us achieves the fertility in the new body that we may have had in the old. We know that surgery is expensive, painful, and risky, yet we take a birth-given physique and with after-market products and services rearrange it for life in the opposite gender role.

Subjective/Objective Disfigurement

I have heard people speak disparagingly of the physical mutilation of sex reassignment, which, if one considers body independent of identity, might be accurate. Certainly, if a man is injured in war and loses his penis, I call it disfigurement. When a woman has a mastectomy in the battle with breast cancer, there is loss and a gain. What some people do not understand, however, and what transsexuals understand too well, is that for us the mutilation occurred first in the womb and second in adolescence. Sex reassignment is the attempt to undo the damage.

Most women don't want a beard, a penis, body hair, a baritone voice, or a receding hair line. Most men don't want to grow breasts, sing soprano, menstruate, and be called "she." I hated my maleness at the ages of five, ten, seventeen, and most days in between, and each new testosterone induced feature compounded the resentment. Likewise, FTMs were displeased with their puberty, periods, and female secondary characteristics. And because the aberration is invisible to others, the suffering is either unnoticed or unbelieved, so transsexuals can't even count on sympathy, let alone treatment. My two-year-old body was deformed because it belonged to a girl; my eighteen-year-old body was deformed because it belonged to a woman. I was trapped inside a living chamber of horrors that no one else could see. (Even Poe could not imagine such a torture.)

On "fixing the body," one transsexual comments:

> There's a feeling of euphoria and freedom that it's hard to describe. Being able to look at myself and not feeling that I was wearing a mask. It's been wonderful. For most of my life growing up I felt I was always hiding. Like when you wear a Halloween mask, you can see your eyes and you know that's you. But it's a façade that you're putting up, and that's how I felt for so long. And now it's just the most fantastic feeling to think, "I'm finished. I'm complete." Yeah. This is how my whole life I've imagined I looked.[25]

Until one understands the deformity, one cannot understand the rehabilitation.

Transsexuals classify genital surgery according to different personal
agendas, and the disparate results of vaginoplasty and phalloplasty are
considerations. Even John Money writes "the success of the female-to-male
sex-reassignment surgery of the genitalia leaves something to be desired,
namely an erectile penis."[26] Creating this "function" is currently restricted
by the fact that the spongy/erectile tissue of the penis is found only in the
penis, so there is no other place from which the tissue can be transplanted.
Yet Money also comments, and my research bears this out, "Throughout
Europe, America, and the English-speaking world, clinicians of transsexualism
agree that a successfully unobtrusive sex-reassigned life is more prevalent in
female-to-male than male-to-female reassignment."[27]

I find it interesting that despite the dramatic qualitative difference of genital
surgery for MTFs and FTMs, reassigned men generally "do better" than
their feminine counterparts. The reasons are elusive, but I believe they are
connected to the qualitative difference in attributed gender.

I talked with and/or received questionnaire responses from about
twenty-five female-to-male transsexuals. One of those was just beginning
reassignment, and was in the full grip of the toughest part of the dilemma –
changing attributed gender. The others reported various stages of genital
surgery, from "none" to "complete," and they had unambiguous male
secondary sex characteristics, lived as men, and expressed masculinity in
different ways. Each considered a penis to be important, but accepted the
surgical limitations as an ordinary part of existence. For example, three
questionnaire respondents describe what it means to be a man:

Inner and outer strength, having provider instincts, being sexually dominant, having
male sex urges . . . wearing conservative male clothes, dating women . . . growing
facial hair, weight-lifting . . . [June 1995]

New clothes, hormones, chest surgery, lifted weights, trim nails shorter, wear beard/
mustache, all new friends (lost lesbian ties), tattoo on arm . . . interest in learning
sports stats, change in mannerisms, walk, tone of voice, self control . . . [November
1995]

Feelings I can "fit in" and be "one of the guys" . . . I am totally perceived as male
and have been since '79 . . . need to be competent and success-oriented in work or
sports settings. [November 1995]

These same men were asked to "Describe the body that would most completely reflect your inner self" and they answered, respectively:

Having a penis and more muscles.

Genital reconstruction, couple inches taller, more body hair.

The body I have now except it would be nice if my penis would fully react and function like the "factory equipped" variety.

The FTMs agreed that having a natural penis would be nice, but none believed that its absence disqualified them as men. The essence of masculinity was themselves. The physics of sexual relations may be altered and require creative compensation, but there is no apparent demasculinized self-image.

I also met three FTMs who were accompanied by their "girlfriends" and one who was accompanied by his wife, and there was no ambiguity between any couple as to who was man or woman, nor did the "genital criterion" disturb their heterosexual characterization of the relationships. Several other men opted not to have phalloplasty "for now," but nonetheless insisted that changing appearance and social status was necessary to maintain sanity. Again, a reconstructed attributed gender speaks more compellingly than genitalia.

Self-concept supported by public recognition creates the man or woman. Along this line, Dr William Reiner comments that in the past there was a predominant trend to reassign "sexually neutral" children as female because doctors could surgically construct a functioning female, but not a functioning male, and "Moreover, many experts believed that a male child could not grow up psychologically healthy without a penis – an assumption not supported by data."[28] My interaction with most FTMs proclaims that they consider themselves "psychologically healthy" men, with or without phalloplasty. My interaction with all transsexuals proclaims that genital surgery is psychologically more important for MTFs than FTMs, and only part of the difference is the comparative quality of vaginoplasty. The greater part is attributed gender.

Eliminating Dysphoria Does Not Eliminate Transsexualism

In *The Uninvited Dilemma*, Kim Stuart offers the concept of the "former transsexual," which she defines as, someone who has had surgery to alter his or her genitals to be more characteristic of persons of the opposite gender... Transsexuals must make many changes to overcome difficult obstacles. Somehow it seems unfair to burden people with labels which no longer seem appropriate when they have made changes, overcome obstacles, made adjustments, had surgery, and taken their places in society in roles in which they are comfortable.[29]

While I find this idea appealing, it seems dangerous to assume that when a transsexual has surgery he or she becomes not transsexual, or even "less transsexual." Sex reassignment is inherently difficult and should be undertaken only when there is no suitable alternative.

Clinical studies demonstrate that psychological therapy has no effect on reversing gender identity. As John Money states, "Psychodynamic psychotherapy is ineffectual... as a cure for the syndrome of transsexualism."[30] Yet it is likewise true that transsexualism is not "cured" after reassignment surgery: genetic sex is not altered; gender role adjustment is not automatically improved; the attributed gender will not be enhanced – if a person has difficulty "passing," that problem will persist; life history is not rearranged, and one does not get to be a little girl by having a vagina constructed in adult life; there is no fertility; and family rejection is not necessarily eliminated or reduced. A foreshadowed "normalcy" after SRS may carry disturbing results, and perhaps even entice some individuals to undergo surgery. Many believe that it will do more than it can. One pre-op MTF told me pointedly, "Now that you've had surgery, you can choose not to be transsexual if you want. I don't have that option – yet."[31] Before SRS, I felt much the same way.

Gender dysphoria is a result of transsexualism, not the other way around. Changing attributed gender and having genital surgery can reduce the gender/body conflict, but it cannot supplant transsexualism, which at this point is medically impossible. The "real-life test" never ends.

I found that many transsexuals had read *The Uninvited Dilemma*, and some stubbornly defended the "former transsexual" concept; however, this came from male-to-female respondents only (about 20 per cent). In my questionnaire, which was designated for "Transsexual Participants," the first question was, "Are you transsexual?" I assumed that this was a throw-away item and the second, "What does transsexual mean?" would bring more colorful reactions. But MTF answers to Question No. 1 include the following:

I no longer consider myself a transsexual.

I am at this point, a transsexual candidate.

No – I am a woman.

No. I was during transition. I feel after completion of surgery, I'm no longer a person in gender transition.

This position is sometimes staunchly defended, i.e., "I've had surgery. I'm a woman." To some degree, life begins at SRS, and everything beforehand is irrelevant. The facts that they may be six feet tall and are often addressed as "sir" do not compromise the invariable proclamation, "I am not transsexual." Militancy may not create reality, but it can be a temporary sanity saver – and it does appear to be temporary. For pre-op transsexuals, a belief in life after surgery helps make the early struggles bearable. This was true for me, because I imagined a post-surgical existence where I would become "normal."

I find the I-am-no-longer-transsexual premise appealing if non-viable. After attributed gender is altered and surgery makes an MTF "indistinguishable" from a natural female, one may want to forget about the reassignment. It is certainly desirable to forget. On the other hand, while it may also be desirable for an FTM, the current state of medical technology does not allow the same opportunity. There remain visible genital distinctions to confirm the presence of the disorder, even if attributed gender is unquestioned. I believe that this is why the I'm-not-transsexual proclamations were from MTF respondents exclusively (if she can fool her gynecologist, perhaps she can fool herself). However, most transsexuals state simply that genital surgery is "icing." Adult reassignment does not lift one from a sex-changed existence.

Kate Bornstein offers an interesting commentary about three "classes" of transsexuals: "Many people divide transsexuals into pre-operative and post-operative, referring to genital conversion surgery. I want to include the option of a 'non-operative' transsexual – someone who doesn't opt for the genital surgery."[32]

Bornstein describes the need of some transsexuals to have surgery as a matter of "comfort point," and some may need to walk a little farther down the road to attain personal contentment (which is understandable). But the concept of transsexuals who do not *want* to alter their genitalia is relatively new to me. There are certainly good reasons for not choosing surgery – medical risk, high costs, poor or mixed results – but until I began this book I never considered that anyone could happily define herself as "a woman with a penis" or "a man with a vagina." Yet I talked with several MTFs who live full-time as women and insist that they will not pursue SRS, not because of financial or medical considerations, but because they are content or pleased with their bodies as they are. One woman stated, "I don't know why god made a girl with a penis, but he did, and he must have had a good reason."

Another, "I just don't think the surgery is worth it. I know what others go through, and I'm pretty happy the way I am." A third, who is distractingly beautiful, described her relationships with men:

> If a man says he loves me, he'd better love all of me. Ain't no part of me that ain't me. Ain't no part of me that's bad. I am an African American heterosexual woman who is transgendered with a penis. How cute. I used to feel sad, sometimes, like I was second class. But no more. A man either loves all of me or none of me. And I mean ALL of me.[33]

What is "All of me?" And how does sex-reassignment surgery play into that concept?

As I mentioned, my psychologist was strict about "standard care" in 1974, even before formal standards were adopted. But I talked with three MTFs who did not start cross-living full-time until after genital surgery. This is a gamble that disables the "real-life test" as a diagnostic procedure and as treatment. One of these individuals has severe psychological problems, self-proclaimed and easily observed, and reports that she was married in the new role, divorced, returned briefly to living as a man, changed jobs several times, became "herself" again, entered a lesbian relationship, started living as a man once more, and plans to have a vaginectomy – all within five years. She lied to her psychiatrists about the cross-living experience because she wanted surgery in order "to *become* a woman."

Gender Cross-Coding

It was once incomprehensible to me that anyone could not *know* his or her gender identity with absolute certainty. But I have met such a variety of personalities who classify themselves as transsexual, and then aren't sure, that I have more respect for the therapist whose patient wants sex reassignment. If the client is not transsexual, there is a danger in taking steps too soon; if the person is transsexual, there is a companion risk of not taking them soon enough.

I have come to see a difference between "gender dysphoria" and "transsexualism" that I did not previously understand, i.e., dysphoria as the effect, and transsexualism as one of several causes. Yet the two terms are often used synonymously. Money discusses gender dysphoria as "the state, as *subjectively* experienced, of incongruity between the genital anatomy and the gender-identity/role . . ., particularly in the syndromes of transsexualism and transvestism"[34] (emphasis added). I know from *The American Heritage*

Dictionary that "dysphoria" means "an emotional state characterized by anxiety, depression, and restlessness"; I know from life that it hurts.

Gender dysphoria is a "subjective" experience, but the cause is objective. This is a key to understanding how a person can be cured of the dysphoria without simultaneously being cured of transsexualism.

Money also lists "gender coding" as "combined genetic coding, hormonal coding, and social coding of a person's characteristics of body, mind, and/or behavior as either exclusively male, exclusively female, or non-exclusively androgynous, relative to a given, and in some instances arbitrary criterion standard"; "gender cross-coding" is "gender coding in which there is discordance between the natal anatomical sex and one or more of . . . *the behavioral variables of male and female*"[35] (emphasis added).

It is interesting that Money denotes gender cross-coding in terms of discordance with the behavioral variables of male and female, as opposed to the variables of men and women. Other writings (some by Money) on the orchestration of behavior in laboratory animals through genetic and hormonal manipulation indicate that observable representations of "gender" can be set in opposition to anatomical sex.[36] By cross-coding the physical development of the brain, behavior is cross-coded. Female rats may exhibit masculine mating responses or male rats may present themselves for mounting if treated with appropriate hormones at crucial times in development; likewise, anatomy can be deviated from genetic sex to achieve varying combinations of genetic, behavioral, and anatomic morphology.[37] The point is that discordant behavioral representations are readily created in laboratory animals. And mice, frogs, hamsters, or rhesus monkeys have no socialized concepts about whether they should wear a dress or a tuxedo, or whether they should call themselves Mary or John. "Gender" is cross-coded by design in laboratory animals. It is cross-coded by happenstance in people. And the physiological determinants are set in motion long before the observable behavioral effects: for example, rats receive hormones *in utero* and behavioral confirmation surfaces in "adolescence." Gender cross-coding defines trans-sexualism, but it is the resulting social and physical restrictions on behavior that precipitate the dysphoria.

In my own case, the associated discomfort grew incrementally worse, though it was not always a steady progression, from my earliest childhood until the age of twenty, when I reached a psychological crisis. In discussing gender-role conflicts for normatively gendered persons (citing Joseph Pleck's *The Myth of Masculinity*), Holly Devor writes:

> It is not uncommon that gender role requirements as outlined in a gender schema conflict with the personalities, talents, and dispositions of growing and changing

people. Such conflicts can result in gender role strain, wherein individuals find it difficult to negotiate their assigned gender role as they understand it . . . In other words, when people do not see themselves as they believe others see them, and as they themselves believe they ought to be, *personality disintegration is possible*[38] (emphasis added).

Gender role is more consensual than gender identity, but each carries heavy constraints. And where role directly opposes identity, personality disintegration is inevitable.

Transsexualism is further complicated in that, while gender identity cannot be reversed, personality is affected by an attributed gender that is discordant with identity through childhood, adolescence, and adulthood. It is safe to assume that a resulting adult concept of femininity or masculinity and its relationship to self will be different from one that had an integrated sex/gender upbringing. If we accept that gender and sex *can* be discordant and that "gender role strain" is real, it follows that such a conflict is likely to cause harm. In fact, I would say it's inevitable; and many transsexuals have reached a psychological crisis by the time they go to a therapist. According to Mildred Brown, "Sooner or later, most transsexuals reach the point where . . . daily functioning becomes difficult, if not impossible."[39] I once told a friend, "Even if transsexuals start out with healthy genders, by the time we go through childhood and adolescence, we're bound to be screwed up." Gender dysphoria is abusive.

As it is important to confirm that the dysphoria is caused by a gender/body conflict instead of neurosis[40] and/or gender confusion, health care workers have a somber responsibility. For now, the "real life test" of cross-living provides the best affirmation. The medical credo of "don't make matters worse" is imperative, but it must be considered from two perspectives. Giving the wrong treatment is harmful, so is delaying the right treatment.

There are reported cases of SRS performed on individuals who are not transsexual, and many have never lived in the opposite gender roles prior to their operations.[41] I visited a surgeon in March 1976 who agreed to perform surgery after a ten-minute conference; there was no requirement for psychiatric screening. His only concern seemed to be $5,200. I had $3,000. A year later, when I could afford the operation, the doctor's medical license had been revoked. And even in the 1990s, I met three transsexuals who obtained genital surgery without completing the real-life test. So there is danger that a non-transsexual may find his or her way on to an operating table.

On the other side, transsexuals sometimes commit suicide. Others report a clandestine self-destructiveness: "Before I started sex reassignment, I tried to drink myself to death;"[42] and some use other drugs with the same intent. Likewise, in the age of AIDS, the corresponding formula of "fucking oneself to death" can have an all too literal meaning. Some transsexuals hide desperately in work and balance two jobs in the deliberate attempt to obliterate every other aspect of existence, even before they begin reassignment and need extra money for medical bills. But mostly, being in the wrong body hurts, and eliminating pain is good.

In her autobiography, Christine Jorgensen writes: "I remember times when I lived in a crucible of troubled phantoms, and faltered in the long, painful struggle for identity. But for me there was always a glimmering promise that lay ahead; with the help of God, a promise that has been fulfilled. I found the oldest gift of heaven – to be myself."[43] "To be myself" requires expression of gender, but it does not apparently require sex-reassignment surgery, even if that added dimension is desirable. Many transsexuals "manage" the discomfort without genital reconstruction. Others say they have eliminated all uneasiness by changing attributed gender (I remain skeptical). But expression of gender is essential.

Theorizing Identity

When I was nineteen years old, after I had been through every kind of self-inflicted masculinity training I could imagine, I quit trying to turn a switch inside my head to say "man" instead of "woman." I acknowledged that the circuit had been welded shut many years before. Yet, still dodging a sex change, I lectured myself: "I am a woman. As long as I know this, it does not matter that the rest of the world sees me as a man."

Outwardly, I stopped acting overtly masculine, and with the exception of dress, I vowed not to deny myself those things traditionally considered "feminine," such as needlepoint, picking wild flowers in meadows, or entering a nursing program. My purpose was to construct a neutral gender role, mostly in an attempt to avoid "macho" comportment, which I could no longer tolerate. I reaffirmed this decision many times, trying desperately to negotiate with my suffering, but within a year I received the first estrogen injection, changed my name, and *never* again contemplated living as a man.

Intellectual definitions of gender identity without visible expression provided no relief. It was impossible to "be myself" without "being a woman," and I was dependent on the rest of humanity for recognition of and interaction with my gender. To pretend otherwise was equivalent to imagining that I could live without food. It takes longer to starve from lack of identity, but the outcome is the same. This was *not* a welcomed assessment.

One of the questions that I asked other transsexuals is "Why is it important that others 'see' your gender as expressed through your body?" The "be myself" formulation was a predominant response:

Well, that is the only avenue we have to display gender. It's in the mind, and only its manifestations, such as clothing, are recognizable to other people . . . [August 1995]

That's who and what I am. [November 1995]

. . . because I'm just being myself. [June 1995]

I think to be accepted. Anyone who is forced to stifle who they are would want to break free. [July 1995]

. . . In a social context, it allows me to express me . . . [November 1995]

To have others confirm what I already know about myself. [October 1995]

Because it allows me to be the male that I am . . . I feel totally free. I was in a cage and now I'm free to be me. [February 1996]

All the changes have been important to me because they have all helped me to become myself. [February 1996]

The inability to be oneself will lead to discomfort. Sex reassignment dispels this impairment. I have never met a transsexual who did not initially try "to be like everyone else" and conform to the social expectations of their birth sex. Some fight decades longer than others.

When asked about her apprehension, a grimly determined, middle-aged MTF who was just beginning hormone therapy answered, "I'm afraid, yes. I may get fired. I may lose my family and friends. But there's no way around it. Pain has overcome the fear."[44] Just as a toothache will send one to a dentist, gender dysphoria will send transsexuals in search of themselves.

5

Shifting Identities

"Real-Life" Dualities

Apprehension and hesitancy about the real-life test are common among transsexuals.[1] The unavoidable revelations and confrontations with land-lords, employers, family, educational institutions, banks, the Social Security Administration, doctors, dentists, credit agencies, the Department of Motor Vehicles, friends, neighbors, and strangers often make the task of changing social status seem overwhelming, especially when undertaken by a person who is already distraught.

With all the obstacles and self-doubt, I am not surprised that some transsexuals try to slip into the new role without others knowing that it is happening. If one chooses the path I did, slamming the door one evening on the male role and opening it the next day on an unabridged female role, the fear and problems must be faced radically, and there is no safe corner in which to retreat when the road inevitably gets rough. So there is a purpose in the attempt to cross-dress in the evenings or at weekends and still maintain a pre-transition job from Monday to Friday. Perhaps it's a way of trying on the new role without giving up everything for it. It also allows partial expression of gender, which may lessen the dysphoria, yet bring other problems associated with a dual life.

I met one woman, age fifty, well-educated, and a teacher, who essentially lives nine months a year as a man, during working hours only, so that she can keep her teaching position; she lives the three months of summer full-time as a woman. She does not know when or if she'll transition full-time, and writes:

> I sought professional counseling . . ., began hormone therapy, changed my name, had a thyroid cartilage shave to reduce my "Adam's apple," and had a bi-lateral orchiectomy to remove my testicles. I have confided in several people at work, although I still present myself as a male there. I have also explained to my mother and, of course, my partner, who has stuck it out with me throughout these many years. I am currently living a bi-gendered life – which is awkward and sometimes

confusing – but seems a good solution at the moment. (Also, I forgot to mention electrolysis to remove facial hair!)[2]

Apparently her physical "configuration" allows her to function in either a masculine or feminine role, depending on the dress and mannerisms she offers to her audience. Since she has not had breast implants or significant breast development from estrogen therapy, secondary female characteristics do not prevent her from sustaining a masculine attribution when she wishes, nor does she need to bind her breasts to compensate. Reportedly she wears a "couple of T-shirts" covered by a loose fitting top when she wants to be perceived as male. Also, since she has not had full genital surgery (only her testes were removed), she is able to urinate from a standing position, which is not important in general social encounters but may be important when one adjourns to the men's room. As I mentioned in Chapter 1, during one of my transitioning washroom encounters, standing to urinate was an overriding cue despite visual impressions.

And yet, in my conversations with her and listening to her speak among other transsexuals, it seems apparent that she considers herself a woman. I am convinced that her gender is feminine, but she finds that shifting roles is an acceptable if unappetizing method of expressing herself, which allows her to keep a job as a man and maintain professional creditability as a non-transsexual. But she clearly does not like to revert to a masculine role at the beginning of the school year. When I saw her in September and October 1995, I mentioned that she seemed "a little down" compared with her usual personality, and that her visible emotional dismay had lasted several weeks. She replied that it is always hard for her to "get back into the male thing when school starts"; nonetheless, she remains determined to "manage" her transition to full-time woman. Reportedly, she hopes to have genital surgery in the summer of 1996, but anticipates working as a man the following year so as not to jeopardize her teaching position.[3]

So if gender itself is not transitory, its recognizable expressions may be. But again, I believe that core gender remains steadfast regardless of any unwillingness to display it or even to reveal it. To support this, in the case of this particular "part-timer," her wife of twenty-five years stated that, even before she discovered that her spouse was actually "feminine," there were tell-tale signs that something wasn't quite right with her "husband." To paraphrase the wife's discovery:

I learned about "Galatea" when I walked in on my husband while he was cross-dressing. After we talked and I found out about the feminine person, many things started to make sense. We have been married many years, but even before I made this discovery, before we began to talk about it and work through it, I often wondered that my husband was just much too nice, too considerate, too polite, too wonderful to be a man, at least like other men I had known. This discovery was not easy for me, because I thought I married a man. But my lifetime with her began to make sense when I finally understood that there was a woman inside the body of my husband. This is a wonderful person. I'm glad I know about her.[4]

Galatea can apparently reverse roles on demand. I find it curious that she retains the ability and that she can endure it. When I left the male world behind, it was a relief, and nothing could make me willingly return to it. And it is significant that she defines herself as a woman even when she functions in the male role, flippantly stating, "Oh, I have to do the guy thing this week." When asked how the above-described changes affected her mental outlook and/or her gender identity, she responded: "I am *much* more relaxed now about the whole issue of gender identity. I still strongly see myself as a woman, but I can function (superficially!) as a male to satisfy society when the need arises."[5]

I met Galatea while she was presenting herself as a woman. She appears convincingly feminine, articulate, and pleasant, with a bittersweet humor, which I find among many transsexuals. I cannot picture her as a man. And she admits that she has to select her wardrobe carefully to pass as male. She comments, "Pierced ears, long nails, lack of body hair, shaped eyebrows, breasts [described as 'small but noticeable'], larger hips . . . make it tougher to play the male role. The beach is out!"[6] Reportedly, she wears lots of loose-fitting sweaters; and because she is balding, that trait overrides many other factors when she does not wear a wig. I also suspect, on the basis of my own experience, that she has less difficulty being accepted as male among people who have always known her as a man, since attributed gender is very hard to change once established. But I would likewise guess, again on the basis of my own experience, that she may be less convincing as a man among people she meets for the first time. She states that the first few weeks of every school year produce questions to school administrators from new students who are apparently confused about Galatea's attributed gender. Perhaps the perceived ambiguity is related to a decreasing aptitude for portraying the male role, perhaps to the physical changes themselves. I suspect both.

Galatea defines herself as transsexual. I define myself as transsexual. Yet we have dealt with the problem through different methods.

I have been surprised in my readings and encounters that not all transsexuals pursue sex reassignment with certainty, though some of the individuals that I have spoken with may not be transsexual. During my investigations, I encountered about twelve people who started reassignment, but I can confirm only two who are continuing. Approximately ten have withdrawn from contact, though they promised not to, and it's my guess that they have discontinued reassignment. One of the twelve, an FTM, remains unreservedly committed and is currently living full-time as a man; another, an MTF, has continued hormone therapy for almost two years, admits that she has doubts, and is searching for ways to minimize the social ruptures of transition; the others, even before I lost contact, seemed to waiver. I was also surprised that some pre-transition individuals specifically sought me out, because I had written *Passage through Trinidad*, and wanted reassurance that all the hassles of a sex change would lead to complete happiness. I was not encouraging; neither is the book.

There is confusion among self-diagnosed transsexuals about the disorder and its treatment, which is complicated by the fact that there is no simple diagnostic confirmation. And since even the most successful transition will bring a lifetime of struggles, it is perversely fortunate that when *minimum* guidelines are followed – psychological counseling, hormone therapy, and the real-life test – only those driven by the deepest suffering will continue the process. And if there are degrees of dysphoria generated by degrees of gender/body conflict, one would expect variation as persons go through, back out of, or "pause" in sex reassignment. One may also expect variations in a single individual before, during, and after transition. For example, I would be embarrassed to wear a mini-skirt at the age of forty-three, but at twenty-three, I often felt sexy and stylish in a tight-fitting skirt that measured 11 inches from hemline to waist; contrastingly, the first time I wore a dress in public I was frightened. Choice of attire and its associated comfort are affected by gender, the willingness to express it, experience in expression, and the approval/reproof one receives. Add gender confusion and role switching, and the measures of transitional progress are compounded.

I have found in my life a heightened awareness of dress as simultaneously liberating and confining – liberating in that it provides an easily recognizable expression of identity; confining in the sense that once a new gender role is successfully established, its ornamental entrapments may become as oppressive as the old. "Galatea" touches on this when she complains: "It . . . irritates me that all women are supposed to look like fashion models!" Yet she adds, "If I am wearing heels, stockings, something short and somewhat revealing, I always get more attention from men. When I wear Levi's and a T-shirt, I become invisible. It is noticeable and predictable."[7]

My own intermittent dissatisfactions with feminine dress do not shake my sense of being a woman. I may grumble about the secretarial uniform or become mildly incensed when my lover insists that I "dress" for a social function, but I will usually slip into pantyhose without undue resentment, and I do not consider myself less of a woman in tennis shoes or more of a woman in pumps. I just think that high heels are inherently impractical, and I avoid them when possible. Compliance with the demands of attributed gender is a weighing of consequences: I like having a job, so I wear clothes that help me keep that job; I like friends and social approval, so I bend my choices to encompass both. When I no longer need an office job, perhaps I'll wear jeans every day. But until then, an occasional dress and makeup aren't unendurable. Sometimes they are delightful, which is perhaps more revealing than my displeasure.

But the entrapments of role are not primary concerns for MTFs who invert attributed gender at will, and role switching seems to provide at least three kinds of relief. The first is a brief respite from the dysphoria; the second is an amusing temporary impersonation; the third is security from full commitment to the opposite gender role. Whatever discomfort we suffer in our birth assignment, it is at least a position with which we are familiar. And for some there is enjoyment in the duality itself: i.e., they want to be perceived sometimes as men and sometimes as women, not as men and cross-dressing men. I do not understand this pleasure, and I generally find it offensive, because it contrasts the real struggles of women in a sexist world against the gamesmanship of role reversal.

Transient Gender Cross-Coding

But it may be that an uncommitted role reflects an "uncommitted" gender. John Money describes an incident where a male-to-female transsexual transiently reverts to a "male-coded personality":

> It occurred when Bertha, a very elegant middle-aged blonde in a red convertible, was sexually harassed by a gas station attendant. Out of the blue, Bertram, the retired military officer, took over, raged at the attendant, upturned him into an empty 44-gallon oil drum, shoved a ten-dollar bill into his back pocket to pay for the gas, and then drove off, triumphantly, as Bertha again.[8]

I, too, encountered a somewhat frightening reversion to "male-coded personality" by a transsexual while I was in the hospital in Trinidad, Colorado. Three MTFs were there at the time I had surgery. On my sixth night of bed confinement, the nurses had difficulty with a newly-admitted patient, "Mr Appleby," who was incoherent and screaming about people trying to kill him. Finally, just as the nurses had quieted the new patient, the transsexual from next door entered my room. I call her "Deborah"; she had

had her surgery one day prior to mine, and was able to get out of bed, while I was still confined. Deborah, a proud ex-marine, began bellowing in response to the commotion. She was wearing a baby-doll style nightgown that hung to mid-thigh, with ruffles around the shoulder straps. I recount the scene in *Passage through Trinidad*:

> "Claudine, what the hell's going on in here? It's 23.30 hours, and people are screaming bloody murder. Is somebody over here bothering you?"
>
> I respond, "They apparently just had an emergency admission; I think the person has had a stroke or something . . .".
>
> "Well, I'm going to find out what's going on. Are you sure no one has been over here bothering you guys? All that noise sounded like it was coming from your room. I'm going to kick somebody's ass if they're over here bothering you."
>
> I'm beginning to get worried now about Deborah, since her aggressive behavior is frightening, and it would be a tough call to determine who is/was yelling louder, she or Appleby. I certainly don't want her to "kick somebody's ass" seven days after surgery, so I try to soothe her because she is intensely angry and her outburst reminds me of a man who's a little bit drunk, a little bit pissed, and a little bit looking for a fight.
>
> "No, no, don't worry about us; we're just fine. Really. It's just that some other patient is having an awfully bad time of it right now. But I know the nurses are with him, and I'm sure they'll handle everything."
>
> "Well, all I know is that it's 23.30 hours and all hell's breaking loose; I thought someone was over in your room causing trouble. Didn't know if I was going to have to kick ass or not, but I wasn't going to sit by and let anybody hurt you."
>
> "We're just fine, really," I assure her. "I think I'll just try to go back to sleep . . . I don't think there's any need to worry."
>
> "Yeah, you're probably right; but if anybody starts messing around with you, just call me. I'm right next door, and I'll cause them a whole lot of grief before I'm done."
>
> . . . Deborah returns to her room.[9]

The image, despite the fact that Deborah was wearing a delicate nightgown, was as intensely masculine as a dramatic come-on from a World Wrestling Federation challenge, only in her case it appeared real. For a brief moment, she was no longer Deborah, but a marine corps soldier who'd fight King Kong with a pocket knife rather than allow somebody to hassle the poor defenseless girl next door. I was surprised to find her chasing windmills at the foot of my bed, and flattered that she would square off unremittingly in my defense. This contrasts with Deborah's self-portrayal earlier that day, when she entered my room sporting a red miniskirt, a white short-sleeved blouse, makeup, jewelry, and pumps, which seemed a natural and well-coordinated declaration. It also contrasts with my enduring image of Deborah as I receive her calls, letters, a photograph, a Christmas card, or when she describes the white dress she wore at her wedding or the heartbreak of the subsequent divorce. I have never seen the "masculine" side of Deborah since the 23.30 incident. I have never heard it in her voice or read it in her correspondence, though I classify her as an aggressive woman. She once reported that she was planning to become male again, which turned out to be a short-lived fantasy. Yet when Deborah deliberately tried to persuade me that she was really a man, she was never as convincing as during those few minutes in Trinidad. I assume that the ex-marine may transiently rise again; and when that metamorphosis occurs, it will not matter whether Deborah is wearing a satin nightgown or a miniskirt with black-knit stockings, there will be no doubt as to who is talking.

In March 1997 I met an MTF who had recently changed her name and, tenuously, her attributed gender. When she met a woman, fell in love, and wanted to get married, she used her birth certificate to obtain a marriage license under her previous name and sex designation. The MTFs partner is reportedly "intermittently male identified," though not FTM, and there is role switching within the relationship. This, again, I find disturbing.

In most instances, I am not sure that true intermittent gender cross-coding occurs, but rather a cross-coding of prescribed gender-appropriate behavior based on (1) discordant gender-role training and (2) ability or self-attributed ability to execute a given behavior. I have often seen actions similar to Bertha's or Deborah's undertaken by natural females who happen to be lesbians. Many told me swashbuckling stories of "kicking ass" or getting their "ass kicked," and it would be easy to assume that they temporarily surrendered to a cross-coded seizure; but since these women reportedly have no gender identity conflict and define themselves exclusively and happily as women, I am not persuaded by gender cross-coding as an explanation. It seems that aggressiveness and/or anger are not exclusive to one gender, that under the right conditions either can respond similarly, and that individuals who have been trained for aggression and who can predict some degree of success will be more likely to undertake it. If Bertha had been raised as a girl from birth and had had a natural female body that stood five feet tall and weighed 95 pounds, I doubt that her anger would have been expressed by attempting to upturn a gas-station attendant into a barrel; I doubt that the idea would occur to her. But if a male-to-female transsexual has not been on estrogens for so long that muscle development has atrophied, if she is six feet tall, is an ex-football star, is strong, weighs 180 pounds, and has been told from birth that physical defense is not only appropriate but is often required, violence may seem a fitting response in certain circumstances. Resulting outrage and response will be contingent on gender, gender role, physical possibilities, and what the person is willing to risk as a consequence. Intense anger may overpower common sense, but in 1973, as a five-foot-five, 120-pound male, I was not about to upturn any station attendants. In 1997, as a five-foot-five female, I would occasionally like to.

Regulated Cross-Coding

Some transsexuals, again a percentage of MTFs only, feel compelled to revert to their prior attributed gender, sometimes even after they have obtained genital surgery, changed official records, and otherwise assumed lives as women. Often the matter is related to work, and I have talked with three male-to-female transsexuals who live as women with the exception of their 8-to-5 jobs. During business hours, they are perceived as men, but they admit that their attempts at masculine presentation are not always stirringly effective. They maintain dual roles because they are afraid that if they leave one job as a man, they'll not find another as a woman, or they'll lose hard-won benefits and seniority, or they'll end up in a low-paying occupation that will set them at the threshold of poverty.

These are the reasons they cite, but for some I question again whether it is an attempt to hang on to the security of a known world instead of stepping too forcefully into a new one. One person admitted pointedly:

And I deluded myself for a while in thinking, hey, you know, if ever – this is just one of those silly things . . ., when everything else blows up in your face, you can always go back to being a man. Well, you can't. You know, and my daughter pointed it out to me one time. She said, "Dad, you don't even look the same." She said, "You don't look the same." And I don't.[10]

And some temporarily resume their prior identities in attempts to hold on to family or friends who they fear may be lost if confronted with the transition. The earlier cited 69-year-old MTF commented that she was planning to "dress male" for an upcoming visit with long-time friends. Part of our taped conversation transcribed as:

Claudine: So, you have been living full-time as a woman for about four or five years? Somewhere in there?

Ophelia: Yeah. Yeah. [*She sounds tired.*] Semi-full-time, because it was still a transitioning period. And I'm still going through that transition. I don't think you . . . really shake it off entirely. Because sometimes there are situations that come up. And as a female, they're not handled well. And it's possible for me now to flip back and take care of that. For example, next week, we'll probably see some friends. We've known them for years and years and years. I knew them in Canada. We were working together. And they still don't know. And we're long friends. But we know that once they know, they'll cut it off just like that. And, they're a couple we respect and admire a great deal, and we hate to lose them. They're Catholic. They'll be shaken to the very foundations. And we will, this time, I'm at a point in my life now where, actually it's very difficult to hide, because if I do dress as a male, I come on very – a very soft male.

. . .

That's what I was saying. These are friends. And I'm going to dress as a male, because if I don't, we will lose them. And I would hate to do that. And for two or three days, I'll live dressed as a male.[11]

This person, as do several others, believes that it is occasionally to her advantage to restore the past attributed gender as convincingly as possible. The reader will notice, however, that the subject does not say that she "becomes a man," but rather that she will "dress as a male," i.e., she sees herself as a woman who will pretend to be a man at a specific time and place and for a specific purpose – something similar, I think, to playing a dramatic role. These are usually short-lived episodes, but not always. Some individuals continue for many years living as a woman in all respects but on the job.

This was a new concept to me, and, before my investigations, I assumed that every transsexual would quit entirely the old attribution at the earliest possible moment. I did not imagine that anyone would willingly bear the strain of switching gender roles more than once.

Coincidentally, the spouse of one of my interviewed subjects asked me if I ever found it necessary to revert to being male. I was startled, but apparently this is a relatively common practice for MTFs, and she assumed that it was sometimes necessary for me. This bit of recorded dialogue transcribed thus (Pandora is the wife; Ophelia, the MTF subject):

Pandora: Has that ever happened to you? When you thought you had to dress [as a male]?
Claudine: I have never.
Pandora: You never regressed?
Claudine: I made the change, the change at twenty. And I never, never turned back.

Ophelia: That was the way to do it. That's absolutely the way to do it!
Claudine: And in a way, I think that may be the easier way, even though you kind of get all the heartbreak all at once.
Ophelia: Yeah.
Claudine: But I've talked to several people who do the switching for family or convenience or necessity sometimes. And I think it would be harder on you emotionally more than anything.[12]

Reviewing my own words, I remain adamant that nothing could ever make me deliberately impersonate a man, and I am surprised other MTFs not only entertain the notion but carry it out.

This is not the case with female-to-male transsexuals. They generally are so antagonistic about having a feminine attributed gender that they do everything possible, even before they take male hormones, to dispense with that attribution and its corresponding role. Most quit wearing feminine clothes and makeup during childhood or teenage years, and certainly by early adult life. FTMs are generally unyielding in their rejection of feminine attire. One man told me, "I got along fine with my parents when I was a child, except when they tried to make me wear a dress. Then there was problems."[13] And although several others reported that they had no particular issue with feminine dress as children since it was expected for many occasions, once they gave up dresses, at whatever time that decision came, they gave them up for good.

One subject showed me a photograph of an otherwise unadorned Christmas tree with seven or eight brassieres hanging randomly from the branches. He explained:

Alex: This is great. I began hormones in January, so I began them six years ago. It took about a year for me to really, I mean, I was like so feminine in a lot of ways, and with my chest and everything, I couldn't bind, so it took me a full year until I was really ready to start transitioning. So I was going to start it actually during the holidays, and I was planning on having my surgery, did have my surgery in April, so I started binding in January, so I didn't have to bind that long. But over the holidays, as soon as I came home and was getting ready to take the Christmas tree down, and I had pulled out my drawer, and I was – I picked up a bra and, "Never gonna have to wear this again," and I chucked it over my shoulder and it stuck on the tree. Meanwhile, my wife started cracking so much, I just started going like this and just started chucking my bras on the tree. [*Laughs*] It's kind of funny.
Claudine: Symbolic.
Alex: Yeah. Very symbolic. The bras went out with the tree that year…[14]

This man is unambiguously male. I do not believe he could successfully change attributed gender on a part-time basis if he wanted, which he clearly does not. And of the approximately twenty-five female-to-male transsexuals I've met, I have never heard one hint that he would be willing to *try* to change attributed gender for work, for friends, or for family. Their force of mind is intense and unyielding, which compares with the relative complacency of their MTF counterparts, even in childhood. One 34-year-old FTM writes: "I was embarrassed about being dressed like a girl. Once, when I was around 8 or 10, my grandmother attempted to force me to sit in a chair, 'like a good little girl,' in a dress, instead of on the floor. She beat me many times that night, but finally gave up."[15]

I questioned this man further during a follow-up interview, since I was surprised he would accept a prolonged beating rather than "sit nice" and wear a dress. He added:

Aunts, uncles, everybody: "She needs to wear more makeup, and you need to leave your hair longer, and you need to boom, boom, boom." You know, but she, my grandmother just . . .[*sighs*]. We're both stubborn. And she even put me in a dress, which is something my mom had stopped doing, 'cause she knew I wasn't gonna wear it. She knew. She understood. Easter? Sure, I'll wear it, tear it up, and go away. And I would, I'd make sure I didn't wear it again. But my grandmother thought, well, my daughter's just not being hard enough on her.[16]

One will not find many female-to-male transsexuals who will accept a part-time feminine attribution once they have reached a physicality where they *can* be attributed as men. I have yet to find one. Even the man who occasionally cross-dresses confirmed that he is perceived as a "fag in drag," which is pleasant – being a boy in a dress is fine; being a woman is not.

Size and Sexism

Related to "perceived" cross-coding is another concept I stumbled on to, quite by accident, in the research. I asked my MTF subjects whether, after successfully changing attributed gender, they encountered treatment as second-class citizens, and if so, were they surprised or was it anticipated. Based on my life experience and the commentary I have heard from natural females, I expected every respondent to answer "yes." I was primarily interested in the types of encounters that would substantiate their enhanced awareness.

I interviewed one MTF who is the managing partner of an electrical engineering firm and who transitioned at that same company. She is a large woman: six-foot-one, about 200 pounds, with an athletic build. She appears at a glance to be strong and forceful, yet her attributed gender seems feminine. When I first talked to her by telephone, her voice was confusingly neutral, slightly deeper than I'd expect from a woman but stylistically and inflectionally feminine (see Chapter 1), and I could not clearly determine attributed gender based on non-visual communication; but when I met her, I immediately accepted her as a woman. She had been on hormones for seven years, and it was three years since her genital surgery. When I asked the second-class-citizen question, to my surprise she stated bluntly that she had not experienced such treatment. She, too, was amazed, because she had assumed that by working in the construction industry, often "on site" in a predominantly male arena, she would find sex-related bias against her, which she has noticed for other women who enter this field. Her conclusion was that because she had been "a really buff male" and continues to be athletic, her robust physical presence compensates for attributed gender and gives her authority. She mentioned that she may occasionally hear a catcall or whistle on the job, but it is rare. This woman expects no nonsense and gets it.

While reviewing her written responses to my questionnaire and especially when talking with her, I noticed that she is supremely confident in her abilities and conveys a notable, almost irritating, lack of fear in social and professional encounters. She understands and *acknowledges* that because of her size and strength, she can easily handle confrontation with a man who might be five-foot-ten and weigh 170 pounds. But underlying her physical strength is a willingness to use it, and this is the element that might be perceived as "gender cross-coding," but should not. And, importantly, she knows that others grasp this as well. She believes that this is part of the reason she does not receive derogatory treatment in the construction industry or perhaps in social encounters.

I now question whether gender-related bias may be, to some extent, a correlative of the average physical size and "presence" of females rather than of the mere fact that they are perceived as women. Could it in part be a "bulk" discrimination as opposed to simple sexism? I checked my notes regarding other MTFs who sent in questionnaire responses or whom I had interviewed to compare the "size" of the individuals with their reported confrontations with second-class status. My notes, though certainly not a large enough sampling, reflected the fact that those male-to-female transsexuals who were noticeably larger than average females, and in fact, were larger than average males, reported that they generally had *not* experienced "inferior" treatment because they were women.

I interviewed another MTF who was six feet tall and about 190 pounds, who also specifically mentioned that she had not encountered treatment as a second-class citizen when she changed attributed gender. Again, this was a surprise to her and me; she also claimed that she had not found many problems during the transition with "people being mean," although this may be in part due to the fact that she currently lives only part-time as a woman. And another male-to-female transsexual, who was about six-foot-four and weighed, I'm guessing, 240 pounds (huge even for a man), reported that she had transitioned on the job, was living and working as a woman, and had experienced no problems with being treated cruelly or disrespectfully. I can't imagine anyone would risk it.

An attributed potential for "fight response" can obviously be affected, and probably diminished, by a feminine attributed gender, but I'm beginning to wonder if sexism may be more of a school-yard-bully-pick-on-the-little-kid phenomenon rather than women-are-inferior, which may be disguised by the fact that females are generally smaller, have less muscle mass, and are perceived as weaker than men. This is part of attributed gender. And gender identity – not attributed gender – also plays a role in the psychological readiness for a fight response. But one fact is certain and pointedly acknowledged by my six-foot-one subject: if a male harasses her, he runs the risk of a prompt, robust and physical response. The sexist man will undoubtedly be aware of this. And there will be no gender cross-coding; "Bertha" will do it all herself.

This contrasts with *petite* or noticeably "pretty" MTFs that I've interviewed, who universally respond to my second-class-citizen question with angry affirmatives, commenting that men will often whistle at them, pinch them on the ass, talk to them as if they (the women) were children, and assume that they are stupid or incompetent, even if the women have educational levels higher than the men with whom they are talking. My 69-year-old subject, an engineer, stated specifically that being perceived as an old woman was very hard for her. By changing attributed gender, she switched from "the privileged position of male engineer" to a "little old lady"; and most people now assume, despite her engineering degree and lifetime of heavy technical experience, that she is helpless, dependent, and incompetent all around. And these "diminutive" transsexuals are also more likely to report physically threatening situations with regard to the transition. They may often be verbally abused in public and confronted in restaurants or shopping centers with derogatory comments about their sexual nature or status. Contrastingly, the middle-aged six-foot-one subject indicated that she could remember only one conversation that disparagingly questioned her sexual status, and it involved comments between a couple talking about her, not talking to her: i.e., the transsexual was apparently not meant to hear. My small-size transition "as I pass"

in 1974, however, brought direct confrontation. I simply assumed that every MTF received this dose of perdition as routinely as taking Premarin.

The passing decades seem to have tempered public response to sex changes, but it may be that relative stature can affect responses during the process. And it seems ironic that the bigger the MTF, the less the chance for abuse, even though her larger stature makes it more difficult to alter attributed gender convincingly in the first place. But that brings up the school-yard-bully theory again.

Still, male-to-female transsexuals, regardless of their differences in size and appearance, are not natural females, and I will leave it to other investigators to determine whether a relationship exists among the general population of women related to body size, a perceived potential for aggression, and sex discrimination. It is a concept that had not occurred to me before I began this book, though I have long believed that gender-role training promotes sexist attitudes in men and women. I now wonder whether physical stature is a significant contributing factor to the discrimination that many women encounter in day-to-day existence – perhaps even contributing more than attributed gender itself.

Trans-Psychosocial Experiences

Optimism

When I was twenty-four years old and soon to graduate from California State Polytechnic University with a bachelor's degree in English, I made an appointment with a career counselor at the university placement office. I was contemplating law school, but wondered how my transsexuality might affect my plans.

During my interview, with a woman whom I remember as professional, restrained, and sincere, there was a disturbing mixture of encouragement and prejudice. I was completely open about my "status," which was rare in 1978; but I wanted to talk earnestly about career options, and since I was to base my decisions on her recommendations, I believed that it was essential to be candid. The counselor handled my disclosure routinely, and we talked for half an hour.

"I am planning to go to law school," I said, "but I am reluctant to spend three years of study when I may never be admitted to the bar. I suspect that I will be prohibited on some kind of moral-turpitude grounds."

The counselor's concurrence was too enthusiastic to be unbiased; but this was the response I expected, so I was neither angry nor unduly disappointed. I reluctantly admired her honesty. After all, she was trying to save me the time and expense of law school when I could never be an attorney. Yet soon after telling me that I was essentially too depraved to be a lawyer, she suggested, "With your GPA, if you had majored in engineering instead of English, we could almost certainly offer placement with several large companies looking for women engineers." When she forgot for a moment that I was transsexual, I was employable; when she remembered, I was not. My search for a meaningful career and personal relationships has been similarly restrained by self-prejudice.

The remarks were inconsequential in themselves. We all, especially women, meet people who are quick to tell us we can't do this or that, offering many reasons why. The significance was that I accepted her evaluation without further discussion with a knowledgeable representative of the state bar or a law school official. And two years later, when my attorney employer insisted that my being transsexual would not preclude admission to the bar, I still tended to believe the counselor.

My personal recriminations have caused me more harm than conscious or unconscious hostility from others. I am forty-three years old, hold a master's degree in English, and have worked fifteen years as a legal secretary. This appears to confuse many people. I have been asked at job interviews, "Why does a college graduate want to be a secretary?" or by friends, "Why remain in a clerical position?" I insist that I like being a secretary, and it provides a base income from which I can do my studying, writing, and thinking without having to publish as a means of earning money. But I carefully omit feelings such as, "There's no need to apply for other jobs, because transsexuals are not hired to fill them." And one of my selection criteria for becoming a secretary was that it was deemed "acceptable" for a woman. If the job did not convey great prestige, it carried a confirmation of my femininity, which was important to me in 1978.

The counselor seemed genuinely sympathetic, though the meeting turned me from a possible course of action. But there is intentional hurt and discrimination against transsexuals. In 1984, an acquaintance described the following incident, which happened to an MTF:

> All the people at work supposedly chipped in to get [the transsexual] a Christmas present. It was beautifully wrapped and given to her at the office party with everyone crowding to watch. When she opened the gift, she found an attractive hardbound book with the title *Freaks* engraved on the cover. Glued on the first page was a mirror. The other pages were blank.[1]

I later met the victim of this "celebration," and was startled that she appeared unambiguously feminine, about five feet eight inches tall, weighing perhaps 130 pounds, with long brown hair, wearing no visible makeup, and dressed in jeans, a man-style blouse, and tennis shoes. She was friendly, mild-mannered, and attractive. How could anyone see a "freak" in this woman? And what kind of people would invent such a prank?

The decision to change attributed gender carries a grave risk of financial and emotional hardship. Sometimes the injury is inflicted intentionally; more often, I think, it comes without overt hostility, but with an ingrained prejudice that may be hard to overcome even for otherwise amiable counselors, employers, co-workers, and acquaintances. And internal bias interplays with external to form a doleful mixture. Quentin Crisp contrasts his lack of industry with an associate's recipe for success:

Never before and seldom since had I witnessed such indefatigability and such singleness of purpose. He wrote and he wrote and he wrote. "I want," he exclaimed in an accent that you could have cut with a sword, "to have behind me a great body of worrrrrk." He was twenty-two at the time. Even had I known that all this apparently fruitless effort would one day lead to his ruling the worlds of radio and television, I could not have followed his example. Industry of that intensity is composed only in part of energy. This I possessed. The rest is optimism, which I lacked.[2]

Optimism on some level is necessary for effort. One way to undermine this faculty is to undergo sex reassignment. A pretty good day is one where I am not rejected, insulted, or assaulted; and by my own conviction, extraordinary success is not possible. The rules of the game exclude it, and the way to avoid disappointment is to avoid ambition. I occasionally readjust my thinking, but after receiving a few copies of *Freaks*, handsomely bound or otherwise, enthusiasm takes a beating. I am a happy secretary.

For two decades I have been a "psychological bag lady," deliberately carrying myself as socially unacceptable – not in appearance, though this has sometimes been the case as well, but through the assumption that it is a foregone conclusion that I will be turned from my objective if I openly confront my transsexualism. Only now, in 1997, am I fundamentally challenging my assumptions. It is no longer quite so important that others may reject me, but important that I should risk rejection. This marks the first step toward Crisp's optimism. There is safety in remaining a secretary, which offers an occupational existence without background checks or notable confrontations. But my worst affliction has been life without hope, so I am forcing a new path to see whether I will become a bag lady in fact.

Transsexual Acquiescence

I was startled in 1992 when I watched *The Silence of the Lambs*. Clarice Starling discusses transsexuals with Hannibal Lecter, and comments: "There's no correlation in the literature between transsexualism and violence. Transsexuals are very passive."

My guess about Clarice's assessment is that most scriptwriters think of the disorder as a male-to-female phenomenon. Sex reassignment is often popularly defined as "men becoming women" in talk shows and "feminist" articles that discount sex changes as a misguided pursuit of the female stereotype,[3] though most sources agree that the FTM/MTF ratio is roughly even.[4] Had Clarice been contemplating the category as a whole, perhaps she would not have defined transsexuals as passive, though I've heard several doctors publicly refer to transsexuals as "gentle and harmless," which may reinforce these assumptions.

I believe this "attributed meekness" is largely based on the compromised images projected by newly transitioning individuals and their inherent cautiousness in testing a new role: for instance, going into the "wrong" washroom at the "wrong" time will draw confrontation; being seen as a boy in a dress on the streets of Los Angeles may attract hostility; and applying for a new job without a convincing attributed gender will meet with a rejection unrelated to competence. I know that I was compulsively passive early in my sex change, and the aim was conscious and specific – to be perceived as a woman. I was afraid to relax the sugar-and-spice boundary, because I feared public ridicule, violence, or arrest if I failed to establish a feminine attributed gender.

Transsexuals are most visible and vulnerable during transition, and I have never met a *newly* transitioning MTF who did not seem acutely reserved in manner, especially if she had just started cross-dressing in public. In the initial stages, "passing" is of the utmost concern; she is terrified of being read. The resulting interpretation may be that she's a transsexual, a transvestite, or a drag queen, but that is not essentially important; the emotional consequence lies in the fact that she is not discerned as a woman. In her attempts to sustain a feminine attribution, she will invariably speak softly (almost whisper) until she learns suitable voice control and inflection, and she may over-dress at casual affairs and be excessively polite. Small steps taken under harsh circumstances may be reasonably characterized as passive; but the resulting societal perceptions gradually disappear as these men and women gain confidence in the new role. Their steps become average. Truer character surfaces when the person no longer thinks about passing, and the contrast in the before and after projections is dramatic.

Similarly, in past decades there has been a tendency to eliminate from gender dysphoria programs those MTFs who did not meet traditional male expectations of women. If the surgical candidate did not demonstrate passivity, acceptance of role, and heterosexuality (in this instance erotic response to males), the person was often excluded as "not a true transsexual." And since patients were aware of this policy, many consciously presented one persona for the doctor and another for themselves; this created a clinical self-fulfilling prophecy that MTFs were "hyper-feminine," which has been documented in much of the literature.[5]

In my contacts with male-to-female transsexuals, I see no predominance of hyper-femininity except during and shortly after the transition period. This was often reported by the subjects themselves. One MTF, who now classifies herself as a "major, in-your-face dyke," briefly adopted a traditional, stereo-typic role after she transitioned. I have never seen anything but the "dyke," who is visible at a glance, in two years. Longer post-transition follow-ups give a better picture of overall gender expression.

There is a different cautiousness in FTMs, though I have not met many that I would describe as passive, even if I would describe them as polite, considerate, sensitive, gentle, and far removed from chauvinists. I met one man just as he made the decision for reassignment. He appeared to be a beautiful and healthy young female who could not be mistaken for anything but a woman. He wore a man's shirt, jeans, and hiking boots, and was clearly female; yet I could almost sense masculinity lurking beneath that fraudulent surface, which was not difficult as he too firmly shook my hand and said, "I am a man."[6] I continue to watch his transformation with great interest. At our first encounter he stated, "I've come to the point where I've got to deal with this problem or go crazy." There was anxiety, intensity, pain, fear, and a compelling hope mixed in the words. The difference I've noticed is not in his stated masculinity, but in the diminishing shame for his body. Initially, his voice would intermittently tremble as he described the inner struggles. Now, his presence says "I am a man" without words. He does not look at the floor when we talk.

I am and have been purposefully self-reserved, with the clear intent of protecting myself from probing questions, but it seems that I perceptually fit the casual description by a fictional character of a non-fictional phenomenon. But I must assume that Clarice's creators have not knowingly met any FTMs, who hardly seem placid, or representatives from the "Transsexual Menace," who are constructively unpassive.[7]

Restructuring Self-Image

Sex reassignment will deliver in the short run and possibly the long run a mixed bodily image, and this is disturbing for most transsexuals. Perhaps it is an inverse of the looking-good, feeling-good proclamations of men and women, who, when dressed stylishly for a date or purposefully for a business meeting, report that they feel powerful, pretty, vibrant, handsome, sexy, or authoritative. But donning a power suit may not erase conflicting mental images or actual ambiguity for transsexuals. Body and clothes work together to confer the look-feel status. One cannot "be" a glamorous call girl until one is first recognized as a girl; one cannot convey the image of a polished executive until one attains a convincing image as a man or woman. There is a difference between an FTM who clothes himself in the hopes of being perceived as a man and another who dresses to make himself more attractive. One posture is apologetic; the other is self-affirming. And an MTF who has not completed electrolysis is unlikely to feel "pretty" at dinner when she and others can see a five-o'clock shadow.

Beauty is in the eye of the beholder, but the self has an eye for it. I remember one poignant remark from an MTF who has been struggling for years to establish a feminine attributed gender. She overheard from across a room, "Who is a pretty woman?" The transsexual whispered sorrowfully to herself, "Any woman." I was not meant to hear, but did. She is reminded each day of her conspicuousness by others and by the mirror.

When transsexuals begin cross-living, dress is often more about alleviating a new-found "mutant" status than showing off the body. Passing is the primary task, and more defiance than celebration: i.e., "I know I look like a man in women's clothes, but this is the best I can do right now." The transsexual has little option but to wait for time, treatment, and learning to strengthen self-confidence and social position. The wait can be a long one.

Again, on the basis of my discussions with approximately twenty-five FTMs, there is little change in dress during their reassignment. The specific exception, though it is not exhibited, is that once these individuals have had a double mastectomy there is no longer any need to bind their breasts, or "chests," as they say. (I don't recall an FTM ever referring to his "breasts," even among those who were very busty as females. The phrasing was always something like, "I had a very big chest, and I hated it!" or, "Binding my chest was painful," or "I couldn't wait to have the top surgery.") All the FTMs wore men's clothes long before they formally began reassignment. Many had lived as butch lesbians, so the change in dress and manner was almost imperceptible, which contrasts with the case of their MTF counterparts, who must modify dress and behavior hand-in-hand with hormone treatments and other procedures to change attributed gender.

I asked, "If I were to look for differences between a very butch lesbian and a female-to-male transsexual who had *not* undergone sex reassignment, what might I find?" One man responded, "I don't think there is that much. I mean, I was pretty much the very butch type lesbian and had met many like myself, and I seriously wondered how much they might be female-to-male and just hadn't come to grips with the fact."[8]

Another FTM, who is a clinical psychologist, told me:

[T]hey know that they're female. I know that they have a sense that there's not incongruity . . . And it was like, yeah, well she's real athletic and she wants to play with the guys, but she is a woman. She is a girl. She knows that . . . And I don't have a desire to do those other kind of things, but I know that I don't feel like she does. And so that clarified for me at a fairly young age that sex-role behavior itself had very little to do with gender identity... Very butch lesbians know somehow, however we know this, that they're women, and they're comfortable with that sense of themselves. And then all the other things that, I think, are very social and cultural or whatever, or even sexual identity issues, are very peripheral to them. And in our society we have trouble with that. We want it to all follow some little pattern.[9]

On the surface, there may be few behavioral differences between a butch lesbian and a heterosexual man. Both may love sports, be sexually attracted to women, cuss like a sailor, drink beer, and smoke cigars; but the one will tell you that she's a woman, the other that he's a man. When in doubt about gender, ask. And for a man who assumes the role of butch lesbian before sex reassignment, subsequent bodily changes invert the public reception of behavior. After reassignment he is perceived as a "normal" male, doing what he used to do as a lesbian. The FTMs notice this difference and enjoy it. They reported that people quit staring at them, heads quit turning when they walked into a room, children stopped pointing at them. They become average as their bodies reset the standards.

Yet it is interesting that a few FTMs were not antagonistic toward traditional female clothing. One stated, "I've worked jobs where I had to wear skirts and nylons and the whole nine yards. No big deal really. I forced myself to do it, but I don't have to any more, and that's great!" He laughed and added, "It gets to the point where it's hard to be a waitress when you have a full beard."[10] For this man, the change in attributed gender eliminated external pressure to wear women's clothes, which was a relief; but those instances in childhood or early adulthood where traditional female dress was required carried no particular meaning.

Another reported that his social change from woman to man happened by accident:

> It was really funny. My first experience at working as a man wasn't chosen. I didn't decide I'm gonna go and apply as a man. I applied as a woman. And I was not a small woman ... But the woman who hired me, and I don't know what she wrote on her paperwork, but when I went to [work] ... I was Bobby, "he." I didn't change it. And that, god, that was a hundred years ago.[11]

This individual has been wearing men's clothes all of his adult life. The change in attributed gender came from hormone-induced transformations. He was surprised and pleased when he unexpectedly became a man in the eyes of others.

"Less Active" Behavior

A routinely accepted image of woman is "less active." There is a reported case of conjoined twin boys who were separated at the age of nineteen months. It is especially interesting from a feminist perspective because the babies shared a single set of external male genitalia along with the liver and some other organs; thus, it was decided that one would be assigned as female and the other as male, and "since one baby was less active than the other, the more active baby should remain the boy."[12] Allowing that the doctors and parents were confronted with two bodies and one penis, the selection criteria may even so have made this child the youngest victim of sexism. On the other hand, how else could this life-shaping decision be made?

One of my first-year psychology texts described "active behavior" as an exhibited difference among boys and girls:

> Even thirteen-month-olds show pronounced differences in reaction to frustration. When the boy is separated by a fence from his mother and toys, he displays active behavior by first trying to climb the fence, then trying to squeeze around it. The girl, in the same situation, bursts into helpless tears.[13]

Passing over the stereotyped "helpless tears," one may ask whether a definitive active behavior exists that can be measured from individual to individual, and if so, is it an earmark of gender? Perhaps at thirteen months children have learned to use different and acceptable expressions of gender *role* to achieve the same end: i.e., if the boy squeezes around the barrier to get to the toys and the girl cries to have the toys brought to her, is it a reflection of core gender or a learned tactic to realize identical ambitions? And further, if active behavior is authentic and gender-specific, it is not gender itself but rather a trait more commonly expressed in boys than girls, and it hardly defines an individual as boy or girl. So given the unlikely mandate of selecting one 19-month-old male to assign and rear as female, active behavior becomes one of the early indications that enable doctors and parents to guess which male might better and more comfortably conform identity to role. If not confronted by this unenviable choice, parents who believe their male child lacks suitable "active behavior" or aggression and/or sexual predation, instead of questioning identity, may look for things like sports or other perceived macho-enhancing methods to bring the behavior up to acceptable gender-role standards.

I spoke with one MTF who learned that she had been born a hermaphrodite, but that since her parents wanted a boy, she had been "corrected" and assigned as male in infancy. This was an incidental discovery made as she gathered early medical records during her psychiatric screening for sex reassignment. I asked how she felt about such a revelation, wondering simultaneously how I might react. Did it make her angry? Did she feel sorrow? depression? bitterness? Did she rage at the social standards that prefer a male child to a female?[14]

She admitted to a combination of ambivalence and anger:

> I don't really think too much about it. At first I was kind of angry, then disappointed. Obviously my parents and the doctors had no way of knowing what the outcome might be. They wanted a boy. I was it. The thing that really bothers me is that my parents went to their graves without ever telling me. I discovered it by accident. The fact that they never told me is more upsetting than the fact itself.[15]

I asked her pointedly, "Do you ever feel bitter because your parents chose your sex for you?" Surprisingly to me, she did not react strongly, but seemed complacent and deliberately accepting. "At first I was upset," she said, "but who can tell? My parents did what they thought was best. How could they know? It might just as easily have worked out, and I never would have known the difference."[16]

It is ironic that this woman, cell for cell the same person, might not be transsexual if she had been initially assigned as female. If she had been given a sex that matched gender, few persons would have known the circumstances. Her physiological ambiguity at birth would not have been reflected in social records or in her own mind, shifted by a mark on a medical consent form. We guess that her life might have been happier, but we know that it would have been different. Physical development, social development, and even gender identity would have been different, modified by a lifetime of "normalcy" and reinforced by a body that unambiguously aligned with her sense of self. And in the absence of a gender/body conflict, there would have been no transsexualism.

Reconciling with Transsexualism

Questions of passivity, perceived or inherent, may change at various stages in the lives of transsexuals. We are aware of our mind/body disharmony from an early age. Reprimands and rewards based on attributed gender are divisive, and we often curse ourselves for conflicts that we did not create. We live with the whole world, ourselves included, trying to make a woman out of a man or vice versa; then we battle the whole world, ourselves included, when we reverse attributed gender and try to reclaim the identity that we fought to suppress. There are mixtures of passivity, resistance, anger, acceptance, denial, depression, confusion, resentment, despair, and joy. To illustrate, I offer the following interview excerpt (with the FTM psychologist):

Claudine: At the first question, I asked, "Are you transsexual?" And you said, simply, "Yes." Some of the transsexuals I've talked to, usually male-to-female, will say that once they've transitioned and they've been through surgery, they are no longer transsexual, they are a woman like every other woman. Do you agree or disagree with that position?

Perseus: Well, I have to disagree with it. And, uh, as far as the thing that they're talking about, and that I see a lot of other guys struggling with, we are not like people that haven't gone through this. Maybe we're more aware of who we are gender-identity-wise than the average person, because we go through so much to express it. But I don't think that a person can ever run away from their past. Our past changes us, affects our development, and it's with us the rest of our lives.

Claudine: Uh-huh.

Perseus: Working with people that are older, who, through the process of life-review and reminiscence, come to integrate and synthesize aspects of their past – for a person to just say, "That never happened" or "I've constructed a new past" or "I'm a woman like everybody else," or "I'm a man like everybody else," to me it shows the enormity of the pain, that they want to move beyond this. And unfortunately, they never will. The issues that we still confront about not being able to reproduce or . . .

Claudine: Go on.

Perseus: Wanting to avoid certain aspects of our past. I know that we don't share that in common with other people. That, in and of itself, makes us different. Whether we want to lie about it or hide it or whatever, it will still be there. Whether it's going to high school reunions, whether it's in talking about grandchildren, whether it's in talking about growing up. And I do get concerned when a person thinks that they can just hide that. Maybe what this other woman's saying – sort of the best thing – where you can say, "Well, I made the best of it, and I'm a better person because of it."

Claudine: Yeah.

Perseus: At least that's some integration. But to act as if it isn't there and that you are like other women or men – you're not. They don't go through this. They weren't socialized like us. And I, I . . .

Claudine: I agree. It's a desirable concept. I mean I would like to think that sometime I would get to a point where I'm not transsexual. It would be wonderful. But it's just impossible – to me. But I've heard, in fact, I've heard that from probably 30 percent of the questionnaire respondents. And I've read in *The Uninvited Dilemma* – the author approaches that kind of thing, the "former transsexual," that once you've gone through this you're not really transsexual, which is a desirable concept, but I don't think it holds up.

Perseus: Well, maybe you're not *per se* like identifying yourself as a transsexual who's going though all these transitions and stages and focused on the transition. But my point is simply on some of the subtleties they're picking out in research in non-verbal behavior. And that as a group it appears that the female-to-males probably could benefit from a little bit of assertion training in certain settings, and that some of the male-to-female folks could benefit from a little bit of being a little bit more toned down, if that's the traits they want to make. But what they're reacting to is their own socialization in the opposite sex that does not, is not consistent with people that didn't go through this. And even something as simple as that, I don't think you can get away from.

Claudine: Yeah. My feeling is, even if we start out when we're born with perfectly healthy formed genders, by the time we go though everything we've gone through, we would be screwed up no matter what. Because we still have to unlearn a lot of things, and unlearn things we have tried to teach ourselves, and unlearn our prejudices that we have formed against being this thing, which I know I had.

Perseus: Well, yeah. And that's something that hardly ever gets talked about. And part of why I do things, a lot of things go into hiding so to speak. And just because we have the affliction doesn't mean that we like it or we accept it.

Claudine: No.

Perseus: Or that we like folks that have this or whatever. There's the real self-hate that goes along with it. Because we are the same. We're the product of the same society and the same culture that grew up thinking, "Well, this is pretty bizarre." And it's why a lot of people, I think, struggle with not accepting the truth about them. Because they don't want to be that.

Claudine: I don't. I still don't. You know, I think I accept the fact, that it's here, and I have to deal with it. But I don't like it, even today.

Perseus: And that's why, I mean, yeah, maybe it's made you and I better people. But if I still had the choice . . .

Claudine: I could live without it.[17]

I spoke on 7 December 1995 with an MTF, about fifty years old, who was also just beginning reassignment. I use the feminine pronoun in conformity with her stated gender, but she looked like a man, and I often had to remind myself that I was talking with a woman. Even so, her "masculinity" was not completely convincing – too soft-spoken, submissive, and gentle for a man; but vague manifestations of gender cannot override the absolute physical presence of "male."

This woman came to me primarily for the emotional support that I could provide as a sex-change "veteran." After knowing her for almost two years, I use the feminine pronoun perhaps 30 per cent of the time to refer to her, which is disconcerting. We have talked for six or seven hours about her childhood, adulthood, inner feelings, and the problems of reassignment. I sometimes react emotionally as if she were a woman; at other times, I react to her maleness. When we talk by phone, I relate better to her gender.

The perception of gender is prejudiced by the body, which is how the gender/sex conflict gives rise to dysphoria, which, in the case of transsexuals, can be unbearable. I am as sympathetic a listener as any MTF could find. With deliberate, sustained effort I attempt to look into her mind, to appreciate character instead of body. But except on the most superficial level, I cannot. The confusion generated by an attributed gender that opposes identity is unmanageable. I believe that I have met a woman who looks like a man, and after several hours of pointed discussion, I am convinced of it. But I will never know "her" until I see the woman I am talking to.

As further background, this person had begun electrolysis seven months earlier, and had been treating herself with estrogens. I urged that she consult a physician, and she has since met with a counselor, obtained a referral to an endocrinologist, and begun supervised HRT. Her comments about dress and her "cautiousness" are especially interesting, because she is a pre-transition MTF. First, the woman has been "shocked" by some transsexuals who "look like men wearing women's clothes," which terrifies her. She explains:

> I know what I look like. And if I wear a dress in public now, I won't be a woman to anybody. I'll still be a man. That's not what I want. I'm hoping to make the change sometime around June [1996]. Hopefully by then I'll look good enough that I can pass. What good is it to go out in a dress if I don't look like a woman? I'll just appear foolish.[18]

For this MTF, again, wearing feminine attire is associated with the desire to be perceived as a woman. Without a corresponding change in attributed gender, cross-dressing will not provide much solace. Many subjects described analogous experiences. And for those MTFs who wear feminine clothes in public before they have convincingly changed attributed gender, or at least obtained a "malleable" attribution, there is the added potential of ridicule and assault.

At some point, cross-dressing is no longer perceived as cross-dressing; actually, the definition of cross-dressing is inverted. A "new man" is wearing men's clothes; a woman is wearing women's clothes. It is accepted by society and, gradually, the individual.

For a professional female impersonator, cross-dressing is a defining behavioral characteristic that makes him transvestic. And to judge by my own experience in the gay community, I long ago lost any ability "do drag." One lesbian friend told me thirteen years ago, "It's too bad you had to be a woman. You would have made a great drag queen." She was aware that I hadn't had genital surgery at the time, but apparently, since I was always perceived as a woman, this disqualified me from associated cross-dressing titles. In another instance, fifteen years ago, a man suggested that it was "a shame" that I changed sex, because he could have otherwise set me up for "good money" as an impersonator-dancer-stripper. "It just wouldn't be the same thing," he added dolefully, although in this case he assumed that I had had surgery.

After twenty-three years of cross-living, I may prefer jeans over dresses, but I am perceived as a woman in either. Denim is more comfortable; dresses are prettier; neither is cross-dressing. And my confidence level regarding attributed gender is the same in either, which marks the significant difference from my pre-transition or in-transition life.

The above-cited woman who is afraid of looking foolish makes no attempt at feminine clothing in public. For now, she presents herself as an attractive, gentle-mannered male, despite her belief that she is and always has been a woman. Privately, she rehearses new manners and new modes of dress, makeup, and hairstyles, indicating that she may first appear in feminine attire at one of the transsexual meetings, where she expects acceptance, support, and critique. I am almost as anxious as she is.

Managing Expectations

Dress is an influential marker of gender, but it is not gender itself. Body is a crucial marker of gender, but it is not gender itself. In those rare instances when psychology and physiology are incongruous, action is taken to realign public expression to suit private experience. Generally, I have found gradations: first, there is a tendency subtly to change dress, sometimes toward androgyny; second, subtly to change manner, sometimes toward androgyny; and finally, to rearrange the body to allow for more dramatic expressions of dress and manner. Gender identity exists independent of sanction by others or self, but gender role is co-dependent on both. The grave decision to act on the body is contingent on some expectation of an improved condition, even if that expectation may be realistically limited.

In *Human Action*, Ludwig von Mises writes:

We call contentment or satisfaction that state of a human being which does not and cannot result in any action. Acting man is eager to substitute a more satisfactory state of affairs for a less satisfactory. His mind imagines conditions which suit him better, and his action aims at bringing about this desired state. *The incentive that impels a man to act is always some uneasiness.* A man perfectly content with the state of his affairs would have no incentive to change things. He would have neither wishes nor desires; he would be perfectly happy. He would not act; he would simply live free from care.

But to make a man act, uneasiness and the image of a more satisfactory state alone are not sufficient. A third condition is required: *the expectation that purposeful behavior has the power to remove or at least to alleviate the felt uneasiness.* In the absence of this condition no action is feasible.[19]

Gender/sex incongruence is uncomfortable. Changing physiology is an attempt to alleviate the "felt uneasiness." Gender is the given, and display is the variable. If a transsexual believes that it is possible to change attributed gender and thereby reduce the dysphoria, a sex change can be pursued. If there is no conviction that public "status" can be altered, suicide may remain as a contemplated alternative; and suicide can be viewed as an attempt to remove uneasiness, one that will succeed in the absence of other options.

The overwhelming reports from my interviewed subjects about the effects of inverting attributed gender, along with its dress and behavioral concomitants, are: "It was right. I became myself." Their consensus is that changing the body is not a changing of self; it is self's inevitable reflection. Despite severe hardships incurred by reassignment (social ostracism, financial burdens, physical pain, and medical risk), the corresponding relief outweighs the consequences. For these individuals, a sex change is logical. It hurts less than a repression of gender.

I asked, "What course do you believe your life would have taken if there had been no cosmetic and/or hormonal treatments to assist in sex reassignment?" Most responses included "I would have committed suicide" (either "pull the trigger" or some variation of "drink myself to death") or "I would have gone crazy." One exception was, "I would have been miserable, but I would have muddled through somehow"; but this person had had a sex change and is happy about it, and she, too, mentioned that she had contemplated suicide. Another said, "I would have lived in hell every day of my life, but I would have lived." Several indicated that they really didn't know what they would have done, but they would have been very unhappy. A few stated that they would have brazenly adopted the lifestyle of the opposite sex and "hoped for the best." Another said, "I likely would have been a fairly hermit-like person . . . I would have felt really terrible that I didn't fit into society . . . the town freak."[20] And Jacob Hale offered:

> It depends on what other depictions we imagine. I mean, in this cultural environment, I don't know . . . because various gender conceptions outside of medicine interact with those in medicine in really close ways . . . If there were different gender categories available to me, maybe I'd be doing something really different. I don't know.[21]

I often asked, "At what age did you know there was a 'problem'?" Almost all transsexuals indicated that they were aware of a conflict by the time they started grammar school, although one MTF reported that she began "noticing a problem at about age fourteen." The earlier-cited, before-transition MTF responded:

> My first really conscious memory was when I was about four years old. I asked my mother if I was a boy or girl. I thought I was a girl, but couldn't quite figure out what was wrong. Anyway, my mother sat me down and told me that I was a little boy. I cried for hours after that.
>   The next day she took me to the barber and had all my hair cut off. I hated that haircut. I figured that was a sample of things to come, so I started trying to be a boy and to forget that I was a girl. It never worked. So here I am, forty years later, trying to learn to be girl again.[22]

Most MTFs acknowledge that clothing is a complement to gender identity, but they want to be seen as women who are wearing appropriate clothes. This doesn't seem to be dependent on whether the person has obtained genital surgery, and attributed gender is vital. I heard from several MTFs who obtained surgery prior to cross-living full-time, and the fact that they have a vagina does not apparently diminish the anguish of intermittently having a masculine attributed gender, nor, as I have mentioned, does a vagina establish attributed gender. One woman, when asked which aspects of her life were the most troubling, responded: "A failed voice surgery has been very disappointing . . . Sometimes I don't pass, people can tell by the way I sound. I'm also very tall . . ."[23]

This is a person who has breasts, a vagina, hormone levels equivalent to those of a natural female, and legal identification that reflects a feminine personage, yet is simultaneously dependent on "passing" to legitimize herself. Attributed gender is not claimed by the militant stance, "I am a woman and don't care what you think!" Rather, it is critically dependent upon the stranger's greeting when one stands in line at Burger King: "Yes, ma'am!" Perhaps there is no therapeutic treatment to alter gender identity, but there is likewise no self-motivational discourse that will make one appear as a woman. And even if it is ultimately established that gender rises from an absolute physiological basis, the related public expression will never be purely biological. It remains subject to one's fellows, and every aspect of human intercourse is preceded by our image as men or women.

Still, the use of "dress" to solidify attributed gender differs significantly for MTFs and FTMs. Most female-to-male transsexuals suggest that "clothing is a non-consideration." FTMs generally wear the same style of clothes after reassignment as before, though one man reported that he bought a "real suit" for the first time, as a kind of celebration after he became "male identified"; and another commented that he purchased several pairs of "good quality pants" when his bodily fat finally hit rock-bottom lean. Most FTMs initially bind their breasts to help secure a masculine attribution, and they generally must cross-live one year before securing authorization for mastectomies, but they pursue that operation with a fervor that rivals an MTF's quest for genital reconstruction. Some wait longer because they cannot afford it, so "binders" may be considered an aspect of dress that assists in transition; but FTMs have long discarded any remnants of women's clothing before reassignment. They simply create a new body for the clothes they wear.

In contrast, dress is crucial in changing attributed gender for MTFs. Estrogens have less dramatic feminizing effects. Many MTFs have male-pattern baldness, excessive facial hair, and low, resonant voices. They may stand six feet tall, carry heavy muscle development, and bear deeply carved features. It is difficult to cross these barriers, even with medical assistance.

Because of this many MTFs *must* use dress to reconstruct attributed gender. By taking time to apply makeup, style their hair or wigs, and pull on a dresses and high heels, they can be perceived as female. Without these endeavors, many cannot.

I commented off-handedly to one woman, "You always look nice! – so professionally and femininely dressed. It really should be an inspiration to do more with my own appearance, but I never seem to put forth the effort any more." She responded emphatically, "I have no choice but to make the effort. If I want to present myself as a woman, I have to."[24]

I asked her, "Do you think there is a problem, generally, with male-to-female transsexuals in learning to dress?" She said, "Yeah. And because many of us start so late, we're trying to make up for lost time. We dress as if we're teenagers."[25] Another MTF, who had been cross-living for eight months and taking hormones for eighteen months, wrote, "During some periods it was necessary to over-accentuate the traditional female dress to pass."[26]

There is a self-acknowledged tendency among MTFs to over-dress during the transition, either wearing ultra-feminine apparel or heavy make-up, though perhaps expertly applied, or dressing "younger" than other women their age. Many report that when they were finally able to wear women's clothes publicly, they "went a little crazy." Their early clothing choices seem to be based on a combination of (1) desperately striving to pass in the new attributed gender and (2) a gluttony of self-expression after decades of famine. Years in the new role temper their selections, as do hormone therapy and/or cosmetic procedures that secure a feminine attribution without special effort.

"Passing" seems to be primarily an MTF construct, and I recall only two FTMs who used that term to refer to themselves; two others used it, but they were referring to male-to-female transsexuals. FTMs generally said that they were "accepted," "recognized," "identified," or "treated" as men. It is certain that FTMs never contemplate a feminine attribution after years of hormone therapy.

Post-Transitional Concepts

Redressing Impersonation

When I was thirty years old I tried privately to impersonate a man. I had moved to a new apartment and discovered a necktie tucked away in a storage box. Hearkening to a dreamlike past, I realized that the tie was mine, the only one I had ever owned, which I wore to the wedding of my closest high-school buddy. I was the best man.

Holding that symbol of masculine authority, touching the smooth polyester fabric, recalling the occasion for which I had purchased it, I almost regretted that I could not put on a suit and tie, step into the world of men, and feel that sense of power that comes from interacting with peers and associates as male – conveniently forgetting my previous frustrations. I undressed and climbed into a man-style blouse and a tan three-piece corduroy suit. This was a clothing combination that I had purchased as a woman and worn without feeling masculine, although I had quit the waistcoat because of its uncomfortable squeeze across my bosom. Next, I draped that rediscovered tie around my neck, struggled briefly to knot it, and slipped into saddle-Oxford loafers that could pass for men's wear. Gazing into a full-length mirror, I was shocked.

There was a woman in men's clothes. My breasts were not effectively hidden beneath the waistcoat, even with a tight jogging bra for extra compression. My long blonde hair looked feminine no matter how I arranged it – loose down the back, pony tail, wound in a bun. The whimsical fantasy of stepping into a man's world was unravelled by the reality of attributed gender; and, though alone, I was embarrassed. Without anticipation I was swept by a wave of guilt, afraid that someone might see my "perversion," and the anxiety was frighteningly reminiscent of when I donned my mother's clothes as a teenager.

I had turned 180 degrees, and felt disgrace at dressing as a man. By surrendering to gender, embracing it through sex reassignment, I inverted the definition of gender-specific dress, even in my own mind. But there is a post-transitional distinction; I remain apprehensive about cross-dressing without a compulsion to engage in it. Once there was dysphoria because I could not be a woman; now there is indifference because I cannot be a man. My new cross-dressing experience died peacefully thirteen years ago.

I talked casually with Professor Jacob Hale on 21 January 1996 about how transsexuals use dress in transition. Hale is unambiguously masculine – perhaps 5 feet and 10 inches tall, 170 pounds, handsome features, a crew-cut, and a tantalizing blend of emotional sensitivity and self-assured arrogance. I formally commented "My preliminary research suggests that dress is less important for FTMs as a factor in changing attributed gender than for MTFs." I jokingly added, "Most of you guys seem to have been defiantly wearing men's clothes since age two."

Hale essentially agreed, but stressed that I was slightly off the mark. "For F-to-Ms, dress is completely irrelevant as a consideration in the transition or after." Five minutes later, however, he unselfconsciously confided, "Well, I finally went out and bought three pairs of good-quality pants. There was no need to do much shopping earlier, until my body was through changing, 'cause I'd buy things and six weeks later they wouldn't fit . . .".[1] He was referring to the progressively decreasing fat distribution about his buttocks and thighs as a result of taking testosterone. So while female-to-male transsexuals may have begun wearing masculine clothing long before reassignment, they are nonetheless aware of how those styles subsequently accommodate body image.

This, again, calls attention to hormone therapy and/or cosmetic surgery. Though FTMs may not modify clothing "form," there is a grand difference in the reception of "masculinity" after transition. The first objective is to be recognized as oneself instead of one's body; the second is to be recognized as an attractive combination of both.

There are few prominent style alterations for FTMs, but there are internal assessment changes when, in the mind of the wearer, clothes begin to match an acceptable gender-specific image. This is reflected in presentation. I asked one subject: "After you started taking hormones, did you notice characteristic changes in your dress and mannerisms?" He responded:

I think I came back more to what my nature was always trying to tell me, in that I grew up in a family where people were very conscious of their outward appearance. And because I was so ashamed – is probably a good word – of how I did look, how I did come across, I really didn't care about how I dressed. I wanted just to wear baggy clothes and cover my body. And as I started into transition, it was wonderful to be able to look in the mirror and say, "Yeah! You look good!" And to actually enjoy shopping for clothes. So that was a dramatic change. And I can't imagine ever going back to how I was before. All these things have made me very sensitive to helping other people. And when I see people who are not concerned about their appearance, sometimes it is rooted in their self-esteem. And just my whole demeanor, I mean, I know that I was always really hunched over, like trying to hide my upper body.[2]

This individual had often worn "boys' clothes" as a child and men's wear almost exclusively as an adult. He transitioned at the relatively young age of twenty, and before that, clothes were used primarily to disguise female characteristics, i.e., wearing "baggy" clothes and "hunching over" to hide breast development. I've heard this from many FTMs. One commented that he didn't discover how long his arms were until after "top surgery," because he previously kept his arms, hands, and shoulders folded over his "chest." But after transition, clothes become an expression of masculinity, a way of "looking good," of appearing sexually attractive, of showing off hairy legs and new muscles, instead of a tactic for hiding femaleness. Similar attire continues to surround what is now a dissimilar body, and a gendered psychology responds dramatically.

The FTM whom I was able to watch transition recalled his surprise and delight the first time a store clerk called out, "Excuse me, sir, you forgot something!" The only outward changes in dress that I have noticed are: (1) a shorter coiffure – his hair was perhaps at the middle of the ear with two or three inches on top when I first met him, which appeared to be gender-neutral, and could have looked good on a man or woman; it was later cut and tapered above the ears in a deliberately mannish style, with perhaps an inch on top; and (2) he also began binding his breasts, which he was not doing at our first encounter. And, of course, during this time he started taking testosterone, which, in about eight months, produced a lowered voice; but the speech patterns and accompanying gestures seem the same, with modestly heavier facial features, and a slightly ruddier, rougher facial skin, though I have noticed no significant beard growth. After three months on hormones, he bragged, "I just got my first pimple." At this remark, another FTM who had long been through this second adolescence said, "It's a rite of passage. But after the twentieth, you won't be so thrilled."

FTMs place greater emphasis on making their bodies fit the clothes. The reversal is contingent on acquiring male secondary characteristics, supplemented by disguising female secondary characteristics – primarily breast binding, at least until the breasts are surgically removed. This varies by individual. Some report that their breasts were small enough to wear baggy outer clothes and tight-fitting underclothes to solve the problem; others, even with binding, had trouble establishing a masculine identity until they obtained the spirit-releasing "top surgery." Some mentioned that binding was effective but torturously uncomfortable, making "it hard to breathe."

And yet many FTMs intermittently adopt traditional feminine dress in an effort to enforce sex over gender. When I asked one man about his understanding of transsexualism, he responded:

> I put a name to it first at fourteen or fifteen when I first read an article in a newspaper, and all of a sudden it made sense. I don't remember, I cut the article out, but I since lost it. I don't remember if it was Christine Jorgensen or who, but I read that this was actually obtained and there was a surgery and it was like, "Yeah." Then I put it all together. And I had approached a couple friends about it and tried to talk to them, and they wouldn't have anything to do about it. They were just totally freaked and didn't want to discuss it. And I think at that point I just started burying it and tried to deny it and went almost the opposite in trying to get away from it. And that's a lot of going by Alexandra instead of Alex. With the jobs that I chose, I'd usually have to wear a skirt and pantyhose, and I'd force myself to do that even though it was completely wrong. I think I did a lot of things that were kind of a way to just keep it buried – and kept it buried for a number of years.[3]

He also mentioned:

> I had slept with a guy for the first time when I was twenty-five, just to see what it was like. [*Laughs.*] And I was starting to kind of hang out with a straight group and trying to fit into that and wasn't . . . I didn't fit into the lesbian community either.[4]

Again, there is frequently an attempt to conform to the gender role of birth, despite inherent feelings that it is wrong. The difference in the FTM approach, however, generally focuses on a strict conformity to dress code. MTFs reportedly ignore dress (although they often vow to stop cross-dressing in private) and focus on going out for sports, getting married, having kids, joining the Marines, or in the words of one subject, trying to "out-macho the guys" so that no one would guess the truth. The methods are inverted when individuals are reassigned and conversely seek to be "good" in new attributed genders.

I have heard more than one post-transition man report, "I am now judged on what I do, instead of how I look." Yet they will in a second breath lament for their MTF counterparts: "How a woman looks is much more important than for a man. Dress is important. Women are scrutinized more."

It does not surprise me that most MTFs devote more time to selection and management of dress during and after transition than FTMs. Women care more because the consequences of not caring are greater. This is compounded for MTFs, who may have difficulty in modifying attributed gender to a point where they are scrutinized as women. Dress enhances the MTF transition and hormones enhance the FTM transition, but each answers to the whole of attributed gender.

Reassessing Physicality

On 6 November 1995 Professor Joanne Eicher sent me a copy of an article that appeared in the *New York Times*, "Size of Region of Brain May Hold Crucial Clue to Transsexuality." The writer cites a study in the Netherlands, which states:

> a region of the hypothalamus, located at the floor of the brain, is about 50 percent larger in men than in women, and almost 60 percent larger in men than in male-to-female transsexuals ... The discovery is the first detection of a difference in transsexual brains and could at least partly explain why such individuals describe themselves as "women trapped in men's bodies."[5]

The article emphasizes that sexual identity is complex, and Dr Dick Swaab cautions, "I'm convinced this is only one structure of many that are involved in such a complex behavior ... This is just the tip of the iceberg."[6]

I enjoyed the news clipping but read it without emotional relief from my own predicament. I filed the information for reference and wrote to Joanne:

> The article tends to confirm something I've known since earliest childhood, although the confirmation won't make much difference in my life. Prejudice is rarely affected by facts. And, to me, this new bit of information is akin to a doctor's running in with the proclamation: "Claudine, great news! Now we understand why you're a freak!" (Well, maybe it's not quite that bad, but that's my gut reaction.)[7]

I may be reassured by the greater understanding and anticipate that it will lead to better and earlier treatment for transsexuals, but for me there remains the undesirable task of being a sex-changed woman. Perhaps the greatest part of gender is the physiology of the brain, but many parts are formed through existence: memories, love of family, childhood, reproduction, holding hands on a first date, going to the prom, feeling pretty, professional relationships, interactions with colleagues, never having to tell someone you love, "I am transsexual," never having to doubt your sanity because you are a woman and your body is male.

I may have always had the brain of a woman, but my body is not an article of clothing that I can exchange for one that is genetically female. And perhaps my socialization was hindered or enhanced by "masculine" training, but life is not ethereal fluff that can be re-created from the present backwards. I am not a full-term woman. Instead, I altered shape from "male" to "femaleness," which is a form that I can compatibly wear and allows others to have a glimpse of me.

The crucial relationship of gender, body, and dress is that unexpressed gender is non-existence. That tiny region in my hypothalamus, smaller than a feminine pronoun, may be a cause, but the effect is that I must be seen as Claudine – the passive construction is important. It is the only way I can be Claudine. Attributed gender is not approval but recognition. We depend on that recognition for our "self"; fortunately, only a few men and women ever have to face that reality or know that it is reality. Life without an acknowledged gender identity is solitary confinement.

Childhood/Adulthood Incongruence

I am dependent on a three-dimensional configuration when interacting with others, and I must interact as man or woman. Femininity is mind, body, and a recognized social status. Even though medical advances and a willingness to use them make it possible for transsexuals to change attributed gender – sometimes flourishingly, sometimes marginally – the outlook for many sex-changed individuals is disheartening. Many transsexuals indicate that, while their lives are improved, meaningful personal relationships often elude them, and they fear exposure of past attributions. A troublesome aspect is the disjointed social upbringing.

In the follow-up questionnaire that I submitted to Dr Biber six months after SRS, I wrote:

One thing that surgery does is solidify the realization that there is essentially no cure for transsexualism; it is a disorder that can be treated, but there is no procedure possible to make me a natural female. I will never be the person I envision I would have been if I had been born female; I can never return to 1953 and start life again; I can never have the childhood of a little girl, the adolescence of a young woman, the family experience of a young bride, wife, mother; I can never have a social history undivided by the change of life from man to woman.[8]

Until medical science can confidently diagnose and treat gender dysphoria in pre-adolescence or early childhood, the prognosis for transsexuals, especially male-to-female, is barren, leaving adult reassignment as a distressing alternative to a more distressing reality. The causes of transsexualism are uncertain, and until there are quantitative and qualitative tests for physiological gender, perhaps based on evidence like that in the *New York Times* article, I doubt that medical practitioners will treat transsexual children by reassignment. The blessing of the child would presumably be easily gained, but not that of the parents or medical personnel, despite the understanding that irreversible steps can be delayed through hormonal management. The afflicted child, with guidance, might begin cross-living to confirm diagnosis and relieve its suffering.

I asked the FTM psychologist whether he had encountered children under the age of eighteen who had obtained treatment for gender dysphoria. He is sympathetic, but responded:

A couple of the people that were referred to me for evaluation were little children, boys that were cross-dressing. And I think that what [the parents] were trying to do is just more of a behavioral intervention, and in one case it did seem like there was probably some family contributors. I've only read about people where the family was supportive enough or the culture was tolerant enough to allow the person to transition at an earlier age.[9]

Several subjects asked their parents for assistance between the ages of ten and fourteen, but were flatly denied, scorned, or taken to a psychiatrist to help "snap them out of it." And usually the doctors were antagonistic toward reassignment. Whether it may be the best thing for the child is generally irrelevant. The best thing for the parents is the guiding factor – understandable for the untrained and unbelieving.

One man said:

I was about age ten, and I said, "Mom, I have something I need to tell you." And I actually, I was like going to confide in her and tell her this incredible secret. By that age, you've learned that it should be a secret ... So I finally told her, "And so, what I want to do is, I want to go to school next year," this was in the summer, "I want to go to school next year as a boy." And rather than her say, "Oh", and be supportive, she said, "Oh, it's just a stage, and you'll get over it." And to have someone dismiss it so quickly, when it took so much bravery, I thought, to finally tell her. That was very painful.[10]

This same individual saved his money and secretly went to a doctor at the age of seventeen. Again, he found no help.

When I was young, probably seventeen, I tried to go to a psychologist in Phoenix, Arizona. He had never dealt with [this], but I just tried to get somebody. And my parents didn't know about it, and I was paying for it with my job. I didn't even put it on my insurance or anything. I took some tests, and he didn't know anything about it, and he just said, "Well, you're too inexperienced. We can't do anything for you."[11]

Most teenage American boys are worried about earning money to buy a used Chevy or take their girlfriends to the prom; this one was concerned about his femaleness. Another explained his bid for childhood reassignment:

I really would have liked to have made the transition back when I was about thirteen. And I came to my mother (my parents were divorced) and said, "You know, I started going into puberty, and this is not for me, and I think I've figured out what's wrong with me." And that is what started, kind of, her taking me to many different mental health people that didn't know what to make of it. A lot of, oh, standard psychological testing, and [they'd] say, "Well, you're not psychotic, and you're kind of bright, so this is just a stage. You'll grow out of it." By the time that I was sixteen, I had been to a psychiatrist that actually told my mother that likely when I became an adult, I would be a guy. But unfortunately nobody would give me hormones or anything at that age. And, uh, [my mother] got real upset and said, "Well, he doesn't know what he's talking about."[12]

So even if a child manages to come in contact with a knowledgeable and caring physician (rare), and even if that doctor believes sex reassignment may be advisable or should be considered through further evaluation, the parents will very probably reject that opinion and search for another who says, "It's a phase. Don't worry about it." Just what parents want to hear; just what I told myself many times.

There are compelling reasons to initiate care at an early age:

1. The changes of the body during adolescence are devastating in that they broaden the gap between gender and sex. The physical deformity becomes greater, and it increases the effort required to alter attributed gender. An adult MTF must nullify masculinization as well as attain feminization in order to pass as female. But if treatment begins before adolescence, hormone therapy can produce secondary characteristics in concordance with gender, eliminating many compensatory surgical and cosmetic procedures, i.e., mastectomy in FTMs and thyroid cartilage reduction, vocal cord surgery, electrolysis, and possibly rhinoplasty and breast implants in MTFs.

2. The longer the social history in a given role, the harder it is to revoke. When a man or woman in his or her mid-thirties undertakes a sex change, his or her attributed gender has been firmly, perhaps irretrievably, entrenched

in the minds of family, friends, co-workers, and the structures of bureaucratic identity – driver's licenses, social security records, birth certificates, credit cards, school files, college transcripts, work history, professional credentials, and so on. It is devastating to re-image this "history" and impossible to reconstruct it.

3. The intense psychological suffering of transsexuals throughout childhood, adolescence, and adult life can be reduced by early diagnosis and treatment. The depth of the pain is reflected in the extraordinary steps that we take to change attributed gender.

In 1973 and 1974 I searched through all the literature I could find about gender identity in an attempt to understand my dilemma and, optimistically, to find a way out of it without reassignment. Unfortunately, I confirmed that a sex change was one of two solutions; the other was suicide. I discovered monographs by two psychologists in the microfilm records at Chaffey College that estimated the suicide rate among transsexuals at 35–40 per cent. Both doctors suspected that the rate was actually higher and hypothesized that many unexplained suicides may be related to unresolved gender conflict: for example, those among people who are apparently healthy, successful, well-liked, and yet kill themselves for no apparent reason. They were referring to statistics that had been collected in the 1960s and early 1970s, and I can attest that there was not much medical help available then.

In 1983, Kim Stuart reported that of her interviewed subjects – generally "successful" transsexuals who survived a sex change – "twenty percent had attempted suicide at one point in their lives. . . . Over one third answered that they would have eventually destroyed themselves emotionally, or committed overt suicide . . . [without treatment]."[13] There is little doubt that the intense suffering that drives us toward suicide can be reduced by early childhood diagnosis and treatment. I also believe that earlier treatment would have relieved much of my contemporary depression and self-revulsion.

4. Gender-appropriate socialization will be enhanced by early treatment; gender-antagonistic socialization will be reduced. This may be a vague concept for many, but it is not for transsexuals. Part of being a woman rests in having the life of a woman. This includes childhood and its associated play, growth, friendships, memories, and family bonds. It includes adolescence and developing secondary sex characteristics that augment gender instead of oppose it. It includes associating with peers and dating from a clearly established feminine attribution. Later there can be marriage and children through adoption, combined with adult varieties of work and pleasure. From early consciousness through to old age, there could be a coherent feminine attribution in harmony with identity. When the congruous rhythm of a

gendered life is broken, there remain many jagged edges. In the words of one man, "Gender role is not a vicarious experience."[14]

5. Early reassignment would decrease the intense suffering of close family members of transsexuals. As I have discussed, there are instances of reassignment and reannouncement of young children because of birth defects, accidents, and hermaphroditism, and their families appear to adjust and come to think of the child in the newly assigned gender. For adult transsexuals this is not possible, and family bonds are often severed, which is difficult for mothers, fathers, brothers, and sisters. One FTM indicated that his sex change resulted in total forfeiture of familial relations, which continues after ten years, and his primary social contact and support comes from other transsexuals. This was basically the reaction of my family, who, rather than gaining a daughter or sister, considered that they lost a son or brother. Twenty years have softened the bitterness, and Mother and Father no longer blame themselves or me[15] for my transsexualism, but they do not know Claudine as a daughter. Predictably, they never will. I am a tolerated remnant of their son.

Familial Identities

With peculiar insight, my mother once said, "If only we had understood when you were younger and got help, perhaps we could have accepted this when you were a child." An after-the-fact prescription, which could not have happened with the medical understanding of the 1950s and early 1960s in the United States; but the comment represents an awareness of her psychic relationship to attributed gender. A mother cannot easily transfer the love for an attributed son, even if she knows that the son was image only. The trick of body is that effigy is reality, and an adult sex change wreaks havoc on *many* lives. We know and love people through our awareness of them. Once the perception of gender is established, right or wrong, it is almost invulnerable. Gender and attributed gender are inseparable from identity.

I have met one mother who appears now to think of her sex-changed "son" as a daughter, but this is an exception, and she admits that the shift in her mind has been difficult. Most transsexuals indicate that their reassignment created grave struggles for others. And the fact that sympathetic family members may want to adjust their perception of a loved one does not guarantee that they will succeed.

Surprisingly, children of transsexuals are the most supportive family group, while siblings are least supportive. Kim Stuart reports in *The Uninvited*

Dilemma that about 50 per cent of spouses and former spouses of transsexuals support the decision for sex reassignment; about 90 per cent of the children of MTFs are supportive as against 66 per cent for FTMs; 26 per cent of siblings support male-to-female reassignments as against 18 per cent for female-to-male; mothers rate at 46 per cent and fathers at 66 per cent for MTF children as against 37 per cent of mothers and 43 per cent of fathers for their FTM children.[16] I did not systematically collect data regarding familial acceptance, but I saw nothing that opposes Stuart's findings. I have been amazed that some family members, especially children of transsexuals, seem so sympathetic, which contrasts with the bitter ostracism sometimes inflicted by the elder members of families.

On the subject of children who accept and love their transsexual parent, I have not met one who likewise started thinking of her father as a mother or vice versa. One girl, about fifteen, proudly introduced me to what I perceived as a rather attractive middle-aged woman by proclaiming, "This is my dad!" And I was told the story of an unambiguously masculine FTM who took his young son to the washroom. As the son was standing at the urinal relieving himself, the boy exclaimed, "Hey, Mom! Let's go to McDonald's." Heads turned in the men's room. Another child, about four years old, whose mother changed from female to male, reportedly created the term "Uncle Mom." This all-too-young girl recognizes the change in attributed gender, but has not lost sight of her mother. One MTF said that her adult children call her "Daddy girl."

And I met one adult son, about twenty-five years old, of an MTF. He uses the term "parent" to refer to his "father." The son said that he "came to a LOTS meeting to support my parent." I talked with him for about ten minutes, asking him about the relationship with his "parent," who appeared to have an unquestioned attribution of "woman." The son told me:

> At first I hated my dad for doing this, back when he first changed. I was so mad and so disgusted I used to go out and beat up other people like that. They all made me sick. I couldn't stand them. But eventually, I got over it, and I love her now. I kid around and wrestle with her sometimes, but she gets mad. Says I play too rough. I thinks she likes it, though. My parent is Blood. That's what counts. If people have anything bad to say about her, and I mean anything, they can accept the consequences – from me."[17]

I asked, half playfully, if perhaps it had been he that I ran into that dreary, long-ago Saturday night. He answered softly but without hesitation, "No. It wasn't me. Probably someone just like me, though. I'm sorry. Those were bad days."[18]

There is a reported case of an infant first assigned as a female, re-announced as a male after nine days, and then seventeen months later reassigned as a female. Despite the initial ambiguity about the child's sex and its sequential designation as girl, boy, girl, her parents and older brother (aged four at the time of the final assignment) quickly adjusted to having a daughter/sister after having had a son/brother.[19] This is not the case in adult reassignments.

As I mentioned, only one parent was so accepting, though I talked with several who would like to be. I met no supportive siblings, and most transsexuals state that they were flatly rejected by brothers and sisters; however, some developed significantly better relationships. One FTM told me that his brother donated semen for artificial insemination of the transsexual's wife; another FTM told me that his brother has offered to donate semen when the transsexual gets married. I encountered several children who thoroughly accept their parent's decision for reassignment, though those same children do not change the parental referent. A mother remains a mother. A father remains a father. And most transsexuals who are also parents are glad that they had children despite the emotional turmoil created by transition. The parent–child bond is difficult to break, and those who have been rejected by their children remain optimistic that these relationships may heal. I believe that it would be better to allow parental and sibling relationships to develop without the challenge of reassignment, better for children of transsexuals (through adoption or artificial insemination) to always know their mother as a woman or father as a man. "Uncle Mom" is a tragic, if loving, term.

Experience as Theory

I have watched my own femininity rise each new day – as a child, as a teenager, as an adult – even when I vehemently fought its ascent. I recognized unconscious manifestations at age sixteen with my first pregnancy dream, yet I hoped "Maybe I only dreamed that I dreamed." Character unremittingly staked its claim. Neither maleness, nor ostracism, nor self-reproach could prevent it.

Differences between men and women are all around us. Some are represented by variant role expectations, but *the* difference is inside us. Gender identity is a primary sex characteristic. It is real. It has a pulse. It wails in three dimensions and in electrochemical substance. Postmodern gender theorists can neither create nor undo this reality.

$\mathcal{N}otes$

Chapter 1

1. Lewis Carroll, *Alice's Adventures in Wonderland* (New York: Avenel Books, n.d.), p. 93.
2. See Holly Devor's *Gender Blending: Confronting the Limits of Duality* (Bloomington: Indiana University Press, 1989). Devor discusses attributed sex and gender. At p. vii she writes, "Sex is generally believed to so strongly determine gender that the two classifications . . . are commonly conflated to the extent that many people use the terms interchangeably and fail to see any difference between the two." I use "attributed gender" to describe an unconscious evaluation of sex and gender.
3. I generally believed that I would be perceived as male until I was ready to be perceived as female. Studies have shown that ". . . when there is doubt as to the gender of an individual, people have a pronounced tendency to see maleness" (Devor, ibid., pp. 48–9). I didn't know this at the time, but I assumed androgyny would leave me as male. This was true most of the time.
4. Mildred L. Brown and Chloe Ann Rounsley, *True Selves: Understanding Transsexualism for Families, Friends, Coworkers, and Helping Professionals* (San Francisco: Jossey-Bass, 1996), p. 102.
5. Male-to-female transsexuals are routinely treated with a combination of estrogens and progestins to suppress androgen secretion, elevate estrogen levels, and replicate the monthly hormone cycle of natural females. Some doctors do not "cycle" hormones in MTF patients and, instead, prescribe regular doses of estrogen over the whole month without progesterone.
6. Panel discussion on "Transgender Human Rights Issues," 15 February 1997.
7. See Ann Bolin's *In Search of Eve: Transsexual Rites of Passage* (New York: Bergin & Garvey, 1988), especially Chapters 10–12.
8. Steven J. Pincus, MD, 13 April 1995, address to LOTS meeting in Irvine, California.

9. Lillian Glass, Ph.D., address to LOTS meeting regarding gender-specific speech patterns, Irvine, California, 13 April 1995. Also see her book *He Says, She Says: Closing the Communication Gap Between the Sexes* (New York: Perigee-Putnam, 1992).

10. Questionnaire responses received on 23 October 1995, and 7 February 1996.

11. Presentation at LOTS meeting, 13 June 1996. Lynn Gold has reportedly practiced in Irvine, California, for thirty years, and specialized in "voice" for the last fifteen.

12. Ibid.

13. Dr James Barrett in "Crossing the Gender Line," an audio tape of a documentary aired on BBC World Service Radio in 1994; he suggests that the ratio is approximately 1 out of every 60,000–100,000 males and 1 out of 100,000–140,000 females. Barrett stresses that these are "broad brush-stroke figures" for the United Kingdom, and world figures are difficult because in many cultures transsexuals cannot readily seek treatment. My estimate is about 1 out of 20,000 for either MTF or FTM. This, too, is a rough appraisal based on the statements of transsexuals about their doctors' reported number of patients as well as published material by and about different practitioners. Stanley Biber, my surgeon, has performed over 3,000 sex-change operations and believes that the ratio of MTF to FTM is about even. About 20 per cent of the MTFs I met went to Dr Biber.

14. I describe the experience in *Passage through Trinidad: Journal of a Surgical Sex Change* (Jefferson, North Carolina: McFarland & Co., 1996). According to Gerald Leve, my endocrinologist, depression after SRS is common. This is also documented by Millie Brown, a counselor who has treated transsexuals for eighteen years and whom I talked with on 7 February 1997. See Brown and Rounsley, *True Selves*, pp. 210–11.

15. For discussion on genetic and hormonal influences on sex and gender see John Money and Anke A. Ehrhardt, *Man & Woman, Boy & Girl: The Differentiation and Dimorphism of Gender Identity From Conception to Maturity* (Baltimore: Johns Hopkins University Press, 1972); also see Devor's "Where It All Begins: The Biological Bases of Gender," in her *Gender Blending*.

16. Quentin Crisp, *The Naked Civil Servant* (New York: Plume-Penguin, 1983), p. 62.

17. Devor, *Gender Blending*, p. 26.

18. Confusion came always from people who did not know me. Once attributed gender was firmly established it was not easily muddled. If

someone knew me as Claudine, I could wear jeans, a sweatshirt, tennis shoes, no makeup, no jewelry, and uncurled hair, and swagger like a fictional cowboy, all without disturbing my attributed gender, although acquaintances might chastise me for being "unladylike." Likewise, on reflection, I cannot think of a person who knew me well as a man who ever effected the mental transfiguration necessary to thinking of me as a woman. A familiar attributed gender and the coincidental attributed sex are difficult to invert.

19. Michael Haederle, "The Body Builder," *Los Angeles Times*, 23 January 1995, E1. Dr Biber was imperiously confident when he explained to me the typical results of his MTF surgeries, and while his attitude was reassuring, I did not believe the result would be that good. A pelvic exam 2½ years later confirmed Biber's skill, as my doctor reported: "The operation was done with exceptional expertise . . . The vagina is indistinguishable from a natural female." Genital surgery does not generally affect attributed gender, but it is important in intimate relationships.

20. Kim Elizabeth Stuart, *The Uninvited Dilemma: A Question of Gender* (Lake Oswego, Oregon: Metamorphous, 1983), p. 116.

21. Friends and acquaintances who knew me as a woman always assumed that I was female; and if they discovered that I had male genitalia, most could not "relate to the idea." I have likewise found, when interviewing a virilized FTM, that I have difficulty conceptualizing a man with a vagina, even when I know that this is the case. See Devor, *Gender Blending*, at p. 147: ". . . in everyday gender information processing . . . gender attributions cause sexes to be attributed."

22. Devor, ibid., p. 119.

23. Jacob Hale, Ph.D., Assistant Professor, Department of Philosophy, California State University, Northridge. This was in Professor Hale's questionnaire responses dated 22 January 1996.

24. Recorded interview (FTM), 16 March 1996, in Irvine, California.

Chapter 2

1. John Money and Anke A. Ehrhardt, *Man & Woman, Boy & Girl: The Differentiation and Dimorphism of Gender Identity from Conception to Maturity* (Baltimore: Johns Hopkins University Press, 1972), p. 128.

2. Claudine Griggs, *Passage through Trinidad: Journal of a Surgical Sex Change* (Jefferson, North Carolina: McFarland, 1996), p. 202.

3. Information about the "transgendered community" is available from

American Education Gender Information Service, Inc. (AEGIS), PO Box 33724, Decatur, GA 30033, and International Foundation for Gender Education (IFGE), PO Box 229, Waltham, MA 02154-0229.

4. Brown and Rounsley, *True Selves*, p. 28.

5. Refer to "A Guide to the Harry Benjamin International Gender Dysphoria Association, Inc.'s Standards of Care," a two-page pamphlet distributed by AEGIS (1995).

6. Ibid.

7. In 1979, California allowed for changing birth records after a sex-change surgery. See *Health & Safety Code* §§10475-10479.

8. The Tennessee Department of Public Health reported to me in 1991: "TN Law: 68-3-203(d) – The sex of an individual will not be changed on the original certificate of birth as a result of sex change surgery."

9. Stuart, *Uninvited Dilemma*, p. 149.

10. John Money, *Gay, Straight, and In-Between: The Sexology of Erotic Orientation* (New York: Oxford University Press, 1988), p. 79.

11. Ibid., p. 88.

12. Stuart, *Uninvited Dilemma*, pp. 124–5. Stuart is a male-to-female transsexual, though she does not admit it in her book. Her more passionate appeal is understandable.

13. Bolin, *In Search of Eve*, p. 65.

14. Recorded interview (FTM), 30 December 1995, in Irvine, California.

15. Brown and Rounsley, *True Selves*, pp. 106–7.

16. Recorded interview (FTM), 30 December 1995.

17. AEGIS, "A Guide to . . . Standards of Care" (see Note 5 to this chapter).

18. Recorded interview (MTF), 17 January 1996, in Orange County, California.

19. C. Jacob Hale, Ph.D., 9 March 1996, interview in Los Angeles, California. It is interesting that Dr Hale made the transition (FTM) in the fall of 1995 while on the faculty at California State University, Northridge.

20. LOTS meeting, 10 April 1997.

21. Paraphrased from my conversation with Gerald Leve, MD, 2 March 1996.

22. AEGIS, "Transsexualism – Sex and Gender Dilemma," Pamphlet (undated, received October 1995).

23. Brown and Rounsley, *True Selves*, p. 134.

24. Gianna Eveling Israel, "Straight Questions, Straight Answers," *TV/TS Tapestry Journal*, 73 (Fall 1995), p. 12.

25. Stuart, *Uninvited Dilemma*, p. 99.

26. AEGIS, "Transsexualism: Sex and Gender Dilemma" (see Note 22 to this chapter).
27. Recorded interview (FTM), 16 March 1996.

Chapter 3

1. Questionnaire responses, 2 August 1995.
2. Questionnaire responses dated 22 January 1996; recorded interview in Los Angeles on 9 March 1996. Professor Hale asked that I identify him.
3. Recorded interview (FTM), 30 December 1995.
4. Money and Ehrhardt, *Man & Woman*, p. 284.
5. Money, *Gay, Straight, and In-Between*, p. 196.
6. Jacob Hale, 9 March 1996, Los Angeles, California.
7. Questionnaire responses (FTM), 7 November 1995.
8. Questionnaire responses (MTF), 27 June 1995.
9. Jacob Hale, 9 March 1996, Los Angeles, California.
10. Stuart, *Uninvited Dilemma*, p. 145.
11. In a 2 November 1995 *New York Times* article, "Size of Region of Brain May Hold Crucial Clue to Transsexuality," researchers report that a region near the hypothalamus is about 50 per cent larger in men than in women and about 60 per cent larger than in male-to-female transsexuals. Gerald Leve, MD, my endocrinologist, citing research currently under way at several universities, predicts that physiological gender will be mapped within ten to fifteen years.
12. See Brown and Rounsley, *True Selves*, pp. 205–9, for more information regarding FTM surgeries.
13. Paraphrased from our conversation on 14 December 1996.
14. Recorded interview (FTM), 16 March 1996.
15. Money, *Gay, Straight, and In-Between*, pp. 35–7.
16. Ibid., p. 36.
17. Anne Moir and David Jessel, *Brain Sex: The Real Difference Between Men and Women* (New York: Delta, 1992), pp. 35–6.
18. See Money and Ehrhardt, *Man & Woman*, pp. 118–23.
19. Ibid., p. 122.
20. Shari Roan, "The Basis of Sexual Identity," *Los Angeles Times/Orange County*, 14 March 1997, E1 and E8.
21. Ibid., p. E1.
22. Ibid., p. E8.
23. Ibid.

24. Money and Ehrhardt, *Man & Woman*, p. 119.
25. Conversation in July 1991.
26. Questionnaire responses, August 1995.
27. See Money and Ehrhardt, *Man & Woman*, pp. 12–13, for a brief discussion on sex "reannouncement" versus "reassignment." If the infant has not yet acquired a sense of gender identity, "one speaks simply of a sex reannouncement"; if they child has begun "to absorb the gender dimorphism," one speaks of reassignment. Distinguishing factors are: "A reassignment requires a change in responses *from the baby*. A reannouncement requires changes in the behavior *only of other people*," i.e., the child is not aware that its attributed gender has been changed.
28. Recorded interview (FTM), 23 March 1996, in San Bernardino, California.
29. Questionnaire responses dated 1 January 1996, and comments paraphrased from our conversation on 11 January 1996.
30. It is especially annoying when an FTM treats me in a condescending manner. This happened rarely, and I am sure it was unconscious. Most FTMs, having grown up with a feminine attributed gender, are sensitive to and antagonistic toward sexism.
31. Griggs, *Passage through Trinidad*, p. 205.
32. From a legal and business perspective, see: David B. Ezra, "Separate but not Equal: Gender-Specific Dress Codes and Employment Discrimination," *Western State University Journal of Law*, 3 (1994) 119–44.
33. Paraphrased from our conversation, 14 December 1995.
34. Recorded interview (MTF), 17 January 1996.
35. LOTS meeting, 13 July 1995.
36. Recorded interview (FTM), 30 December 1995.
37. LOTS meeting, 9 May 1996. This is paraphrased from my notes.
38. Money and Ehrhardt, *Man & Woman*, p. 13.
39. Ibid., p. 178.

Chapter 4

1. Money, *Gay, Straight, and In-Between*, p. 34.
2. Ibid., pp. 33–4.
3. Ibid., p. 34.
4. Ibid.
5. Ibid, p. 12.
6. Irvine, California, 14 December 1995.
7. Questionnaire responses, 22 January 1996.

8. Recorded interview (FTM), 30 December 1995.
9. Ibid.
10. Questionnaire responses, 5 February 1996.
11. Ibid.
12. Recorded interview (FTM), 16 March 1996.
13. Paraphrased from my conversations at an "Under Construction" meeting, 21 January 1996.
14. Irvine, California, 30 December 1995.
15. Biber mentioned this during one of his bedside discussions when I had surgery; also see John Tayman, "Meet John, er, Jane Doe," *Gentlemen's Quarterly* (December 1991), p. 299.
16. Tayman, ibid.
17. Conversation, 10 April 1997. This is paraphrased from one of the men who spoke at "FTM Night" at a LOTS meeting, which was designed to increase awareness among MTFs about the FTM transition.
18. See Bolin, *In Search of Eve*, p. 50. Her discussion of the Standards of Care *circa* 1980 includes the diagnostic elements: "A. Sense of discomfort and inappropriate about one's anatomic sex. B. Wish to be rid of one's own genitals . . ."
19. The decision to have surgery isn't equivalent to the desire to have a vagina or a penis. Most transsexuals would prefer a "factory equipped" body if they could magically obtain it, but their choice is to have or not have genital surgery, with the associated costs and risks.
20. Recorded interview (MTF), 17 January 1996.
21. Recorded interview (MTF), 6 January 1996, in Irvine, California. Six months later this woman underwent sex-reassignment surgery in Belgium.
22. Recorded interview (FTM), 30 December 1995.
23. Tayman, "Meet John, er, Jane Doe," p. 223.
24. These three FTMs have not had genital surgery, although one had a hysterectomy. The first comment was made on 21 January 1996; the second is from questionnaire responses received 21 January 1996; the third is from questionnaire responses dated 22 January 1996.
25. "Crossing the Gender Line," an audio tape of a documentary originally aired on BBC World Service Radio in 1994.
26. Money, *Gay, Straight, and In-Between*, p. 92.
27. Ibid.
28. Roan, "The Basis of Sexual Identity," p. E8.
29. Stuart, *Uninvited Dilemma*, pp. 4–5.
30. Money, *Gay, Straight, and In-Between*, p. 96.
31. Paraphrased, 18 April 1996. This was a response to my off-handed

comment that I resent being transsexual. I met several MTFs who similarly objected to my use of the term.

32. Kate Bornstein, *Gender Outlaw: On Men, Woman, and the Rest of Us* (New York: Vintage, 1995), p. 121.

33. These three quotations are paraphrased from conversations at a LOTS meeting, 9 November 1995.

34. Money, *Gay, Straight, and In-Between*, p. 201.

35. Ibid.

36. See Money and Ehrhardt, "Fetal Hormones and the Brain: Effect on Sexual Dimorphism of Behavior in Animals," in *Man & Woman*, pp. 65–91.

37. Ibid., pp. 24–35 ("Genetic Dimorphism").

38. Devor, *Gender Blending*, p. 60.

39. Brown and Rounsley, *True Selves*, p. 96.

40. I use "neurosis" in the generic sense of an emotional disorder; and transsexuals may have problems distinct from gender identity issues.

41. See Stuart, *Uninvited Dilemma*, pp. 14–15 and 113–15.

42. This sentiment was reported by about twenty individuals and seemed evenly divided between MTFs and FTMs.

43. *Christine Jorgensen: A Personal Autobiography* (New York: Paul S. Eriksson, Inc., 1967), p. 332.

44. LOTS meeting, 14 December 1995.

Chapter 5

1. Stuart, *Uninvited Dilemma*, p. 99.

2. Questionnaire responses (MTF), 1 August 1995.

3. She had surgery in July 1996 and continues, as of April 1997, teaching as a man. It will be interesting to see how her "bi-gendered life" progresses.

4. Conversation of 14 December 1995. This is loosely paraphrased because the wife used both masculine and feminine pronouns – masculine when she referred to her husband by "his" name; feminine when she referred to her sex-changed partner by "her" name. I have tried to capture the essence of the dialogue, which was heartfelt.

5. Questionnaire responses, 1 August 1995.

6. Ibid.

7. Ibid.

8. Money, *Gay, Straight, and In-Between*, p. 76.

9. Griggs, *Passage through Trinidad*, p. 120.

10. Recorded interview (MTF), 17 January 1996.
11. Ibid.
12. Ibid.
13. Paraphrased from unrecorded conversation, 21 January 1996.
14. Recorded interview (FTM), 30 December 1995.
15. Questionnaire responses (FTM), 23 January 1996.
16. Recorded interview (FTM), 23 March 1996.

Chapter 6

1. This was related to me in 1984. I met several MTFs in 1984–5, and their "horror stories" reaffirmed my decision to keep my past hidden.
2. Crisp, *The Naked Civil Servant*, p. 88.
3. See Germaine Greer's chapter, "The Stereotype," in *The Female Eunuch* (New York: Bantam, 1971), pp. 51–60.
4. See Stuart, *Uninvited Dilemma*, p. 20, referring to Dr Paul Walker's commentary. Stanley Biber stated, "There are just as many women who want to become men as men who want to be women . . ." – see John Tayman, "Meet John, er, Jane Doe," *Gentlemen's Quarterly*, December 1991, p. 299. Also, I distributed 75 questionnaires to transsexuals through different group meetings, my endocrinologist, and subject-to-subject referrals. Eighteen completed questionnaires were returned to me – nine from FTM respondents and nine from MTF. However, the 100+ transsexuals that I met were weighted toward the MTF side by about four to one. I attribute this to the facts that (1) FTMs generally transition very effectively and can hide in a new life if they choose; and (2) FTMs are more guarded about their pasts. This seems directly related to greater peer rejection associated with men, i.e., the FTMs' male peers are less tolerant about this subject; thus, it is easier for MTFs to find compassion among their female friends than FTMs among their male friends and associates. Most of the FTMs admitted that they would never have talked with me, had it not been that (1) they wanted to tell their story – the literature often ignores the FTM transition; and (2) I am transsexual and they trusted me to maintain confidentiality.
5. For a more detailed discussion, see Bolin, *In Search of Eve*, at pp. 106–20.
6. This may seem a strange thing for a person to say. But prior to sex reassignment, the only clear indication any third person has of discordant gender is the statement from the afflicted individual. Our conversation occurred at a meeting of transsexuals, so this man felt

confident in discussing the matter. But if he had not said, "I am a man," I would not have known.

7. I spoke with one representative of Transsexual Menace at the UCI Bridges of Courage conference (14–16 February 1997). The group does not actually define members as "a menace," but because transsexuals are frequently perceived as such, they purposefully react to the label. The group includes both MTFs and FTMs.

8. Recorded interview (FTM), 30 December 1995.

9. Recorded interview (FTM), 30 March 1996.

10. Paraphrased, 30 December 1995.

11. Recorded interview (FTM), 23 March 1996.

12. Stuart, *Uninvited Dilemma*, p. 152.

13. Jerome Kagen and Ernest Havemann, *Psychology: An Introduction* (New York: Harcourt Brace Jovanovich, 1972), p. 379.

14. According to Money and Ehrhardt, *Man & Woman*, it "appears that the prejudices of physicians skew today's hermaphroditic sex reassignment statistics in favor of a change from girl to boy . . ." (p. 154).

15. Irvine, California – paraphrased from our conversation (MTF), 14 December 1995.

16. Ibid.

17. Recorded interview (FTM), 30 March 1996.

18. This is paraphrased from a conversation on 7 December 1995. I made notes afterward but did not record the dialogue. As of April 1997, she has not begun the cross-living test.

19. Ludwig von Mises, *Human Action: A Treatise on Economics* (London: William Hodge, 1949), pp. 13–14.

20. Recorded interview (FTM), 30 March 1996.

21. Jacob Hale, 9 March 1996, Los Angeles, California.

22. Paraphrased MTF, 7 December 1995.

23. Questionnaire responses, October 1995.

24. Paraphrased MTF, 8 February 1996.

25. Recorded interview (MTF), 6 January 1996.

26. Questionnaire responses (MTF), 5 February 1996.

Chapter 7

1. Paraphrased from my conversations with Hale at an "Under Construction" meeting. There were about fifteen FTMs there, and the group reportedly has about sixty members.

2. Recorded interview (FTM), 30 March 1996.

3. Recorded interview (FTM), 30 December 1995.
4. Ibid.
5. Natalie Angier, "Size of Region of Brain May Hold Crucial Clue to Transsexuality, a Study Finds," *New York Times*, 2 November 1995, p. A12.
6. Ibid.
7. Letter dated 12 November 1995.
8. The entire questionnaire and responses are reprinted in Griggs, *Passage through Trinidad*, pp. 196–203.
9. Recorded interview (FTM), 30 March 1996.
10. Recorded interview (FTM), 16 March 1996.
11. Ibid.
12. Recorded interview (FTM), 30 March 1996.
13. Stuart, *Uninvited Dilemma*, p. 125.
14. FTM, 30 March 1996.
15. Parents sometimes blame themselves, asking, "What did I do that made my child this way?" Another troubling aspect is that people may blame the victim. I heard many transsexuals cite comments like: "If you loved us, you wouldn't be this way," or "If you tried harder, you could accept your role," or "It's your duty to suffer and not tell anyone," or "You're perverted, and we want nothing to do with you." Several transsexuals were told that it would be more dignified to commit suicide than undergo a sex change. This is emotionally devastating.
16. Stuart, *Uninvited Dilemma*, pp. 23–5.
17. Irvine, California (paraphrased), 13 March 1997.
18. Ibid.
19. Money, *Gay, Straight, and In-Between*, p. 72.

Select Bibliography

Angier, Natalie. "Size of Region of Brain May Hold Crucial Clue to Transsexuality, a Study Finds." *New York Times*, 2 November 1995, p. A12.

Bolin, Anne. *In Search of Eve: Transsexual Rites of Passage*. New York: Bergin & Garvey, 1988.

Bornstein, Kate. *Gender Outlaw: On Men, Women, and the Rest of Us*. New York: Vintage, 1995.

Brown, Mildred L., and Chloe Ann Rounsley. *True Selves: Understanding Transsexualism for Families, Friends, Coworkers, and Helping Professionals*. San Francisco: Jossey-Bass, 1996.

Crisp, Quentin. *The Naked Civil Servant*. New York: Plume, 1983.

Devor, Holly. *Gender Blending: Confronting the Limits of Duality*. Bloomington: Indiana University Press, 1989.

Ezra, David B. "Separate but not Equal: Gender-Specific Dress Codes and Employment Discrimination." *Western State University Journal of Law*, 3 (1994), No. 1, pp. 119–44.

Glass, Lillian. *He Says, She Says: Closing the Communication Gap between the Sexes*. New York: Perigee, 1992.

Greer, Germaine. *The Female Eunuch*. New York: Bantam, 1971.

Griggs, Claudine. *Passage through Trinidad: Journal of a Surgical Sex Change*. Jefferson, North Carolina: McFarland, 1996.

Haederle, Michael. "The Body Builder." *Los Angeles Times*, 23 January 1995, pp. E1 and E5.

Israel, Gianna Eveling. "Straight Questions, Straight Answers." *TV/TS Tapestry Journal*, 73 (Fall 1995), 11–12.

Jorgensen, Christine. *Christine Jorgensen: A Personal Autobiography*. New York: Paul Eriksson, 1967.

Kagen, Jerome, and Ernest Havemann. *Psychology: An Introduction*. New York: Harcourt Brace Jovanovich, 1972.

Moir, Anne, and David Jessel. *Brain Sex: The Real Difference Between Men and Women*. New York: Delta, 1992.

Money, John. *Gay, Straight, and In-Between: The Sexology of Erotic Orientation*. New York: Oxford University Press, 1988.

Money, John, and Anke A. Ehrhardt. *Man & Woman, Boy & Girl: The Differentiation and Dimorphism of Gender Identity from Conception to Maturity*. Baltimore: Johns Hopkins University Press, 1972.

Roan, Shari. "The Basis of Sexual Identity." *Los Angeles Times/Orange County*, 14 March 1997, pp. E1 and E8.

Stuart, Kim Elizabeth. *The Uninvited Dilemma: A Question of Gender*. Lake Oswego, Oregon: Metamorphous, 1983.

Tayman, John. "Meet John, er, Jane Doe." *Gentlemen's Quarterly*, December 1991, pp. 221–7 and 299–300.

Von Mises, Ludwig. *Human Action: A Treatise on Economics*. London: William Hodge, 1949.

Index

active behavior, 119
Adam's apple, 27
adrenogenital syndrome, 54, 70
Alex (pseudonym), 32, 67–8, 81–2, 85, 107, 132
Alice's Adventures in Wonderland, 1
"ambisextrous," 48
American Educational Gender Information Service, 27, 143–4n3
androgens, 5, 9, 34, 82, 130
"androgyny," 28
anorexia, 37
antiandrogens, 34
attributed fertility, 63
attributed fight response, 110
attributed gender, 1, 6, 14, 17, 19–20, 25, 29, 38–40, 54, 59, 61, 71, 75–7, 79, 86, 91, 100, 129, 134, 138, 142n18
  ambiguity, 3, 14, 15, 18, 20–22, 116
    changed attribution by single observer of single subject, 21–2
    tendency to see male or male-to-female, 20, 141n3
    mixed images, 116–17
    unpredictability of attribution, 18, 20, 118
  androgyny as attribution, 20
  barrier to identity, 54
    effigy is reality, 138
    in MTF before transition, 122–4
  fragmented attributions, 73
  handshake contract, 6
  inverted social expectations, 1, 14, 50–2, 59, 63, 71–3, 77–8, 102, 132
    attributed gender dominant over "genitalia," 72–3, 79, 143n21
    job-related, 51–2

inverted social reception of gender, 78, 132
  post-transitional confidence, 124
no dual attribution for single subject, 66
no perceptual middle ground, 1
official recognition, 29, 40–1
past attributions, 7, 105
  difficult to invert, 100, 142n18
  photographs, 64, 67
  relationship to self, 42, 116–18, 125
  SRS does not affect, 91, 126
  transition, 6, 15, 19, 130–3
    discontinuing reassignment, 100–1
    euphoria, 41
    full-time/part-time, 24, 98–102
    managing expectations, 124–8
    more effective in FTMs, 86, 89
attributed heterosexuality, 71, 73, 77–8
  reconstructed heterosexuality, 77–8
  sex change and same lovers, 74, 77
attributed homosexuality, 71, 73, 79
  inverted homosexuality, 77–8
attributed meekness, 115
attributed sex, 19, 25, 71, 76, 141n2, 143n21
  penis, 87
attributed sexuality, 71, 73, 79
  reconstructed sexuality, 77–9
aversion therapy, 47

Baghdad, 17
Belgium, 35
Benjamin, Harry, 27
Beverly Hills, California, 16
Biber, Stanley H., 15, 25, 39, 82, 86, 134, 143n19
biographical editing, 8
birth certificate, 28–9